Published by Reyes Therapy Services

Paperback ISBN: 979-8-9964426-0-7

Hardcover ISBN: 979-8-9964426-1-4

Contact: eric [at] reyestherapy [dot] org
www [dot] reyestherapy [dot] org

This book is for educational and informational purposes only and is not a substitute for professional mental health treatment, diagnosis, or medical advice. Reading this book does not establish a therapist-client relationship with the author. If you are experiencing psychological distress, seek support from a qualified licensed mental health professional, such as Eric Reyes, LCSW.

Author’s note

Before you begin this book, I want to explain why I wrote it the way I did. I could have written this in a more academic voice, more technical, formal, and emotionally distant. There is a place for that kind of writing, but it was never the kind of book I wanted to put into someone’s hands. Because the truth is, most people reading this are not lacking information. You have probably already spent years trying to understand yourself. You may already know the language of anxiety, trauma, mindfulness, emotional regulation, attachment, or overthinking, yet there is often still a gap between insight and freedom. Between understanding yourself and actually living differently. That gap is why this book exists.

As a psychotherapist, I repeatedly noticed the same pattern in people. Many understood their struggles intellectually yet still felt trapped by their own internal experiences. They became highly skilled at managing themselves while still organizing their lives around fear, avoidance, emotional discomfort, self-doubt, or the constant need to feel “okay” before fully engaging with life, and that realization became the foundation for the

Transcendent Functioning Model.

Part of my thinking was influenced by Abraham Maslow's later ideas surrounding transcendence and the possibility that human growth extends beyond self-actualization alone, but my interest eventually moved in a different direction. I became more interested in what transcendence looks like psychologically in everyday life

What allows someone to continue moving toward meaning, growth, connection, and values even while experiencing anxiety, uncertainty, grief, intrusive thoughts, or emotional pain? At its core, TFM is about learning how to feel fully without being controlled by what you feel.

That is also why I chose to self-publish this book. I wanted the writing to remain direct, emotionally honest, and more human than clinical. While the ideas are grounded in evidence-based psychology, especially Acceptance and Commitment Therapy (ACT), mindfulness, and psychological flexibility, I intentionally wrote this in a more accessible and emotionally grounded way rather than as a purely academic text. In many ways, I consider it semi-academic.

You may also notice the language throughout this book feels different from traditional psychology or self-help writing. That is intentional. I was less interested in simply giving information and more interested in creating moments of genuine self-recognition while reading. Some of the language is intentionally reflective and emotionally immersive because I wanted the writing to speak not only to the analytical mind but also to the deeper internal experiences many people struggle to articulate even to themselves.

I also encourage you to pay close attention to the valuable case studies presented in Chapters 11 and 12. While the cases are presented as hypothetical, they are deeply informed by years of clinical experience working with individuals facing anxiety, depression, trauma, OCD, emotional avoidance, and chronic psychological struggle. All identifying details and circumstances have been altered or generalized to fully protect confidentiality. This book is an invitation into a different relationship with yourself. So, as you read this, try not to approach it like information to consume. Approach it honestly and pay very close attention to the parts that make you uncomfortable or resistant. Those moments often point toward something much more important. —*Eric Reyes*

Table of contents

Introduction

Most people who pick up a book like this have already tried the usual stuff. They've done the breathing exercises. They've journaled. They've maybe gone to therapy, read the self-help classics, and downloaded the meditation apps. And some of it helped, at least for a while. The anxiety got quieter. The bad days became less frequent, and life felt more manageable. But manageable isn't the same as free.

There's a gap between feeling less bad and actually living well. Between keeping your head above water and swimming somewhere on purpose. Most of the tools people learn are designed to close the first gap. They're built to reduce suffering, and they do that reasonably well. The problem is that reducing suffering and building a meaningful life are two completely different projects, and almost nobody tells you that. This book is about the second project.

You're here because you've sensed that something bigger is possible. You've had glimpses of it. Moments where you were completely locked in, fully present, acting from a place of clarity instead of panic. Moments where the noise in your head went quiet long enough for you to actually show up as the person you know you can be. You want more of that. You want it to be the rule, not the exception, and that's exactly what this book is built to give you.

Welcome to the Transcendent Functioning Model

For decades, the dominant goal of mental health work has been symptom reduction. Identify the problem, treat the problem, and measure whether the problem is smaller. That approach has helped a lot of people, and it shouldn't be dismissed. When someone is in genuine pain, relief matters. Getting stabilized matters. You can't build anything on a foundation that's crumbling. But here's what the research and real-world experience keep showing: Symptom reduction alone doesn't produce a rich life. It produces a quieter one, and there's a difference.

Think about what it actually looks like to organize your whole psychological life around avoiding distress. You start making decisions based on one question: Will this make me feel worse?

You skip the high-stakes presentation because the anxiety might spike. You avoid the hard conversation because it might go badly. You turn down the opportunity because the uncertainty feels too heavy. Each individual decision seems reasonable. But over time, your world gets smaller. You're not choosing your life anymore. You're managing it. And the exhausting part is that you're doing everything right, following all the advice, using all the tools, and still feeling like you're running in place.

That's the trap that symptom-focused thinking creates. It makes the absence of discomfort the definition of success. And since discomfort is a permanent feature of being alive, you end up in a permanent state of vigilance, always scanning for the next threat, always one difficult emotion away from feeling like you've failed.

The Transcendent Functioning Model, or TFM, starts from a different premise entirely. It says that psychological well-being isn't the absence of struggle. It's the capacity to live fully in the presence of struggle. It's the ability to feel the anxiety, the self-doubt, the grief, and the frustration and still move toward what matters. Not because the difficult feelings go away, but because they stop being the deciding factor.

This isn't a repackaging of positive thinking, and it's not about convincing yourself that everything is fine when it isn't. TFM draws from some of the most well-supported ideas in modern psychology, particularly acceptance and commitment therapy and mindfulness-based practice, and extends them into something more complete. It gives you a model for operating at a higher level, not just a set of coping tools. In that sense, it aligns with approaches that emphasize psychological flexibility, present-moment awareness, and values-based action rather than mere symptom reduction.

The model describes three distinct levels of human functioning. The first is *reactive functioning*. At this level, your internal states run the show. When you feel anxious, you avoid. When you feel unmotivated, you stop. When you feel overwhelmed, you shut down. Your behavior is essentially a direct output of whatever emotion is loudest at any given moment. Most people spend more time here than they realize.

The second level is *regulated functioning*. This is where most traditional self-help and therapy aim to get you. You've learned techniques to manage your emotional states. You can calm yourself down, reframe negative thoughts, and interrupt a spiral before it takes over. These are real skills, and they matter. But regulated functioning still keeps your internal state at the center of the equation. You're managing the weather instead of being controlled by it, which is better, but you're still watching the sky constantly.

The third level is *transcendent functioning*. At this level, you're not trying to control the weather at all. You've transformed your attention from your internal state to your values and the actions those values require. You can feel the storm, acknowledge it clearly, and still steer the ship. Your execution doesn't depend on how you feel. Your consistency doesn't collapse when things get hard. You operate from a stable core that isn't rattled every time your emotions transform.

That third level is what this book teaches you to reach.

Consider someone like Jordan, a hypothetical 29-year-old graphic designer who's been dealing with anxiety for most of his adult life. He's tried therapy, read widely, and built a solid morning routine. His anxiety is lower than it used to be. But he still hesitates before pitching his own ideas in client meetings. He still spends Sunday evenings dreading Monday. He still holds back creatively because the fear of judgment feels too loud. His symptoms are managed. His life, though, hasn't expanded. He's regulated, but he's not free. TFM is built for people exactly like Jordan, people who've done the work to get stable and now want to know what's possible beyond stability.

What You Will Learn and Why It Matters

This book is structured around a specific and testable idea: that your ability to execute, create, connect, and contribute doesn't have to be tied to how you feel in any given moment. You can decouple your performance from your emotional state. Not by suppressing what you feel, but by changing your relationship to it so completely that it stops having veto power over your choices.

That transformation doesn't happen by accident; it requires understanding exactly why the old approach keeps failing and then replacing it with something that actually works at the root level. You'll learn why fighting your thoughts makes them stronger, not weaker.

There's a well-documented psychological phenomenon, sometimes called the paradox of thought suppression, where the more energy you spend trying to push a thought out of your mind, the more central it becomes.

It's the same reason telling yourself not to think about something makes you think about it immediately. Traditional symptom management often works against this principle without realizing it. The more you try to eliminate anxiety, the more your brain treats anxiety as a serious threat worth monitoring. TFM teaches you to stop fighting and start observing, which is a completely different relationship with your own mind.

You'll also learn why inconsistency isn't a character flaw. It's a structural problem. When your ability to act depends on feeling ready, motivated, or calm, you're building your entire system on the most unreliable foundation possible. Emotions are designed to fluctuate. They respond to sleep, to blood sugar, to random memories, to the weather. If your consistency depends on your emotional state being cooperative, you're going to be inconsistent. Permanently. The solution isn't to try harder to feel better. The solution is to build a system that doesn't require your emotions to cooperate.

You'll understand the three levels of functioning in real, practical terms. Not as an abstract theory, but as a map you can use to locate yourself in any situation and know exactly what to do next. When you're *reactive*, there's a specific set of moves that help. When you're *regulated*, there's a different set. And when you're building toward *transcendent functioning*, there's a clear path that gets you there and keeps you there.

The reason this matters goes beyond personal performance. The people who struggle most with inconsistency, with fragmented thinking, with starting strong and fading fast, aren't lacking intelligence or desire. They're lacking a coherent internal structure that governs how they think, decide, and act when things get hard. Without that structure, every difficult emotion becomes a potential derailment. Every stressful week becomes a reason to restart. Every setback resets the whole cycle back to zero. This book gives you that structure.

You'll stop consuming information and start

integrating it. One of the most common patterns among the exact people this book is written for is what might be called overconsumption without integration. You read the books, watch the videos, absorb the ideas, feel a surge of clarity and motivation, and then watch it fade within days. The problem isn't the quality of the information. The problem is that information without a unifying system doesn't stick. TFM gives you the unifying system. It's the thread that connects everything you already know and makes it usable.

The Path Ahead: Core Processes and Ultimate Freedom

TFM is built on four core processes. Each one addresses a specific mechanism that keeps people stuck at the reactive or regulated level. Together, they form a complete architecture for transcendent functioning.

The first process is *cognitive defusion*. This is the practice of separating yourself from your thoughts, not by ignoring them, but by seeing them clearly for what they are. A thought is a mental event. It's not a command. It's not a fact. When you're fused with a thought, you experience it as reality. "I'm not capable enough" feels like a true statement about who I am. Defusion lets you step back and see it differently: "*I'm having the thought that I'm not capable enough.*" That gap between you and the thought is where your freedom lives. Defusion doesn't silence the inner critic. It strips the critic of its authority over your behavior.

The second process is *experiential expansion*. This is about widening your capacity to feel without being overwhelmed. Most people have a narrow window of emotional tolerance. When feelings get too intense, they either shut down or act out. Experiential expansion stretches that window. It teaches you to sit with discomfort, to feel anxiety without fleeing it, to feel grief without drowning in it. This isn't toughening up in the old-fashioned sense. It's developing a more spacious relationship with your own inner life so that difficult emotions become something you can hold rather than something that holds you.

The third process is *attachment reduction*. This one is subtle, but it might be the most important. Attachment reduction is about loosening your grip on the idea that things need to be a certain way before you can function well. The attachment to feeling confident before acting. The attachment to having certainty before deciding. The attachment to being in the right mood before showing up. *These attachments feel protective, but they're actually the chains.* When you reduce them, you stop waiting for the right internal conditions and start moving regardless of them.

The fourth process is *intentional action.* This is where everything else lands. Defusion creates space. Expansion builds tolerance. Attachment reduction removes the conditions you've been waiting for. Intentional action is what you do with all of that space and freedom. It means moving toward your values on purpose, consistently, even when the internal weather is rough, and not because you've conquered your emotions, but because your actions are no longer held hostage by them.

These four processes don't operate in isolation. They build on each other and strengthen each other in ways that become clearer as you work through this book. Defusion makes expansion easier. Expansion makes attachment reduction possible. Attachment reduction makes intentional action consistent. And consistent intentional action, over time, produces the kind of life that most people only glimpse in their best moments.

The deeper lesson running through all of it is this: *true psychological well-being isn't the absence of struggle.* It's the capacity to live fully while struggle is present. The storms don't stop. The difficult thoughts don't permanently disappear. The anxiety, the doubt, the grief, and the frustration are part of being human, and no model that promises to eliminate them is being honest with you. What changes is your relationship to all of it. You stop being a person who is buffeted by internal weather and become a person who can navigate it with skill and intention.

By the time you reach the end of this book, you won't just understand these ideas intellectually. You'll have a clear, specific set of practices that build each process into your daily functioning. You'll be able to identify which level you're operating at in any given situation and know exactly how to move toward the transcendent level. You'll have a stable internal structure that doesn't collapse under pressure, doesn't require perfect emotional conditions, and doesn't reset every time life gets hard.

That's what operating above your emotions actually looks like. Not detachment and numbness. Not the absence of feeling. It's full presence, full awareness, and full commitment to what matters, regardless of what your internal weather is doing on any given day.

The science is real. The practices are specific. The outcomes are achievable, and the work starts now.

Chapter One

Beyond Symptom Reduction: The Call to Flourish

Most people who seek help with their mental and emotional lives have one goal in mind. They want to stop feeling bad. They want the anxiety to quiet down, the low moods to lift, and the racing thoughts to slow. And that makes complete sense. When you're in pain, relief is the most natural thing to want. Nobody walks into a difficult week thinking, "I hope this teaches me something."

You just want it to stop, but there's a problem with making "stop feeling bad" the finish line.

When your entire strategy is built around reducing symptoms, you end up organizing your life around the very thing you're trying to escape. Every decision gets filtered through one question: will this make me feel worse? You start avoiding situations that might trigger discomfort. You pull back from conversations that feel risky. You turn down opportunities that carry any uncertainty. Slowly, without realizing it, your world gets smaller, not because you chose to shrink it, but because you were managing it.

That's the trap, and it's one of the most common traps that smart, self-aware people fall into.

The Trap of Traditional Management

Traditional approaches to emotional and psychological difficulty tend to focus on management. Manage your stress. Manage your triggers. Manage your anxiety. The word itself tells you something. You manage a problem you don't expect to solve. You manage a condition you've accepted as permanent. Management is a maintenance strategy, not a growth strategy. And for a lot of people, it becomes the ceiling instead of the floor.

Think about what symptom-focused management actually looks like in daily life. You learn to recognize when your anxiety is rising, and you apply a technique to bring it down. You notice a negative thought spiral starting, and you interrupt it with a reframe. You feel the tension building before a hard conversation, and you use a breathing exercise to calm your nervous system.

These tools aren't useless. They genuinely help in the short term. But if those tools are your entire strategy, you're spending a huge amount of mental energy just staying even.

You're running to stand still.

There's a concept in psychology called the hedonic treadmill. It describes how people tend to return to a relatively stable level of emotional experience regardless of what happens to them, good or bad. When you win something big, you feel great for a while, then return to baseline. If you lose something important, you feel terrible for a while, then return to baseline. The treadmill keeps moving, and you stay roughly in the same place. Symptom management works in a similar way. You feel bad, you apply a technique, you feel better, and then something else comes up, and you're back at the start. The cycle repeats. Month after month. Year after year. And the frustrating part is that you're doing everything "right" and still feeling stuck.

This isn't a failure of willpower. It's a failure of the model.

Consider someone like Marcus, a hypothetical

34-year-old marketing manager who has spent three years working on his anxiety. He's read the books. He's tried therapy. He meditates most mornings and keeps a journal. By any measure, he's doing the work. And yet he still dreads Monday mornings. He still avoids the high-visibility projects at work because the pressure feels too intense. He still turns down social plans when he's had a hard week, not because he doesn't want connection, but because he doesn't trust himself to show up well. His symptoms are lower than they used to be. But his life hasn't expanded. If anything, the constant monitoring of his internal state has become its own source of exhaustion.

Marcus isn't broken. He's just been playing a game designed to keep him at zero instead of helping him get to ten.

The problem with symptom reduction as a primary goal is that it creates what researchers call experiential avoidance. This is the pattern of organizing your behavior around escaping or minimizing uncomfortable internal experiences. And the cruel irony is that the more you avoid an uncomfortable feeling, the more powerful it becomes. Psychological research has shown this repeatedly. When you try to suppress a thought or push away a feeling, it tends to come back stronger. The act of avoidance signals to your brain that the thing you're avoiding is genuinely dangerous, which makes your brain monitor for it even more carefully. You end up more sensitive to the very thing you were trying to get rid of.

There's also a deeper cost that's easy to miss. When your psychological energy goes toward managing your internal state, it can't go anywhere else. The person who spends significant mental bandwidth scanning for anxiety triggers, applying calming techniques, and recovering from difficult emotional moments has less capacity left over for creative work, for genuine connection, for bold decisions, for the things that actually make life feel worth living. They become, as one way of putting it, an expert in their internal landscape but a stranger to their external one. The inner world is tightly monitored. The outer world quietly shrinks.

This is what psychological fragility looks like in practice. It's not dramatic. It doesn't announce itself. It just shows up as a life that keeps getting a little smaller, a little safer, a little more defended. You stop pitching the big idea. You stop reaching out first. You stop signing up for the thing that excites you because the risk of feeling bad feels too high. And because each individual choice seems reasonable in the moment, you don't notice the pattern until you look up one day and realize how far you've drifted from the life you actually wanted.

The language of symptom management can quietly pathologize normal human experience, too. Sadness after a loss is natural. Nervousness before something important is natural. Uncertainty when you're trying something new is natural. When those experiences get treated as problems to be fixed rather than signals to be understood, you lose access to the information they carry. You also start to believe that feeling anything difficult means something has gone wrong, which makes you more reactive to difficulty, not less. The goal stops being to live fully and becomes simply to avoid feeling bad. That's a significant narrowing of what a human life can be.

Chapter Two

Defining Transcendent Functioning

Transcendent functioning is a different proposition entirely because it doesn't ask you to feel better before you start living. It asks you to start living and let the feeling follow, or not follow, as the case may be. The goal transformations from managing your internal state to engaging with what matters to you, regardless of what your internal state is doing at any given moment, are crucial.

This is a bigger transformation than it might sound.

When your goal is to feel good, your life becomes organized around your emotional comfort. When your goal is to act in alignment with what you value, your life becomes organized around something much more stable. Values don't fluctuate the way emotions do. Your value of honest connection doesn't disappear when you're anxious. Your commitment to creative work doesn't evaporate when you're tired. Your care for the people around you doesn't vanish when you're having a hard week. Values are durable in a way that emotional states simply aren't. Building your functioning on values instead of feelings is like switching from a foundation of sand to one of stone.

"Transcendent functioning," as a concept, draws from some of the most well-supported ideas in modern psychology. Acceptance and Commitment Therapy, often called ACT, has done significant work in this area. It defines psychological flexibility as the ability to contact the present moment fully as a conscious human being and to move toward what matters, even when difficult internal experiences are present.

TFM takes that idea and extends it. It treats psychological flexibility not just as a therapeutic outcome but as the central operating mechanism for a high-functioning life. Think of it this way. A skilled sailor doesn't control the ocean. The ocean is going to do what the ocean does. Waves will rise. Storms will come. The wind will transform without warning. What the sailor controls is how they respond to all of it. They read the conditions, adjust the sails, hold the course when possible, and adapt the route when necessary. Their destination doesn't change every time the weather changes. Their commitment to reaching it doesn't waver every time a wave hits the hull. They've developed the skill to navigate, not the power to stop the sea.

Your internal world is the ocean. Thoughts will arise that you didn't choose and don't want. Emotions will surge at inconvenient moments. Old fears will show up before important events. Doubt will whisper before big decisions. None of that is going to stop. What changes, through the practice of transcendent functioning, is your relationship to all of it. You stop trying to calm the ocean and start getting better at sailing it.

The transformation from internal battle to outward engagement is what makes this different from traditional management. In management mode, the primary question is, "How do I feel right now, and what do I need to do about it?" In transcendent mode, the primary question is, "What do I value, and what does that value ask of me right now?" The first question keeps your attention locked on your internal weather. The second keeps your attention on your direction. And where your attention goes, your life follows.

This doesn't mean your feelings become

irrelevant. Transcendent functioning isn't about becoming emotionally flat or detached. Your feelings carry real information. Anxiety can signal that something important is at stake. Sadness can signal that something meaningful has been lost. Anger can signal that a boundary has been crossed.

The difference is that in transcendent mode, you can receive that information without being dictated by it. You can feel the anxiety, note what it's telling you, and still choose your response based on your values rather than the emotional pressure. The feeling becomes data, not a command.

Consider a hypothetical scenario: someone like Priya, a 27-year-old graduate student who has struggled with social anxiety for years. In symptom-management mode, Priya's goal before any social event is to get her anxiety low enough that she can function. She runs through calming techniques, tells herself reassuring things, and monitors her internal state carefully throughout the event. If the anxiety spikes, she feels like she's failing. Her entire experience of the event is filtered through the question, "Am I okay right now?" In transcendent mode, the goal transforms. Priya acknowledges that anxiety is probably going to show up, and she decides in advance that its presence won't determine her behavior. She goes to the event because she values connection, not because she feels calm. The anxiety is still there. But it's no longer running the show.

That's the practical difference. Not the absence of difficulty, but the absence of difficulty's authority over your choices.

The Engine of Psychological Flexibility

Psychological flexibility (Hayes et al., 2006) is the mechanism that makes transcendent functioning possible. Without it, the gap between knowing what you value and actually acting on those values stays wide. With it, that gap closes. Understanding how flexibility works and how to build it is one of the most useful things you can do for your own functioning.

Flexibility, in this context, means something specific. It's the ability to be fully present with whatever is happening internally, without getting so caught up in it that it controls your next move. When a difficult thought arises, a flexible mind can notice it without fusing with it. When a difficult emotion surges, a flexible mind can feel it without being swept away by it. When circumstances change unexpectedly, a flexible mind can adapt without losing its sense of direction. This isn't a personality trait you either have or don't have. It's a set of skills that can be learned and strengthened through practice.

One of the most important components of flexibility is what ACT calls cognitive defusion. When you're fused with a thought, you experience it as reality. The thought "I'm going to fail at this" doesn't feel like a thought. It feels like a fact. And facts demand a response. If failure is certain, the logical move is to stop trying. Defusion breaks that automatic chain. It creates a small but significant gap between you and the thought, a moment of recognition that says, "This is a thought my mind is producing, not a direct report on reality." That gap is where choice lives.

Imagine standing at a train station watching trains go by. Each train is a thought. In a fused state, you don't watch the trains. You get on every single one, immediately, without deciding to. You end up wherever the thought takes you. Defusion is learning to stand on the platform. You see the trains. You can even read the destination signs.

But you get to decide which ones you board. The trains don't stop coming. Your relationship to them changes.

The second component is what TFM calls experiential expansion. Most people have a relatively narrow window of emotional tolerance. When feelings get too intense, they either shut down or act out. Experiential expansion is the practice of widening that window. It's not about enjoying difficult feelings. It's about being able to hold them without immediately needing to escape them. When you can sit with discomfort without fleeing it, you gain access to a much wider range of choices. You can have the hard conversation even when it feels uncomfortable. You can stay in the creative process even when it feels frustrating. You can hold uncertainty without immediately needing to resolve it through avoidance.

The third component is present-moment contact. This sounds simple, but it's genuinely rare. Most people spend a significant portion of their mental life either replaying the past or rehearsing the future. Rumination and worry are both forms of time travel that pull you out of the only place where action is actually possible: right now. Present-moment contact means bringing your attention back to what's actually happening, what's actually being asked of you, and what's actually available to you in this specific situation. It's not about clearing your mind. It's about choosing where your attention goes and bringing it back when it wanders, which it will, constantly.

These three components work together. Defusion loosens the grip of unhelpful thoughts. Experiential expansion builds your capacity to feel without being overwhelmed. Present-moment contact keeps your attention in the place where your values can actually guide your behavior. Together, they create the conditions for what might be called committed action: moving toward what matters, consistently, even when the internal weather is rough.

Think about a musician performing on stage. They don't play a perfect concert by eliminating nerves. They play a good concert by developing the skill to keep playing even when nerves are present. A wrong note happens. A good musician doesn't stop the performance to process the wrong note. They feel it, absorb it, and weave the next note into something that works. The mistake becomes part of the music rather than the end of it. That's exactly what psychological flexibility allows you to do with your own internal experience.

It's worth saying clearly: building psychological flexibility, like playing an instrument, takes practice. It doesn't arrive as a sudden insight. The people who develop it do so through repeated, deliberate engagement with difficult internal experiences rather than repeated avoidance of them. Every time you notice a thought without immediately acting on it, *you're building defusion.* Every time you stay present with an uncomfortable feeling instead of escaping it, *you're building experiential expansion.* Every time you bring your attention back to the present moment instead of letting it drift into rumination, *you're building present-moment contact.*

The research behind these ideas is substantial. Steven Hayes and colleagues at the University of Nevada developed the ACT model over several decades of clinical research, and the evidence base for psychological flexibility as a predictor of well-being and functioning is now extensive.

Studies have found that higher psychological flexibility is associated with better mental health outcomes, greater work performance, stronger relationships, and more consistent goal-directed behavior. The mechanism isn't mysterious. When you're not spending your cognitive and emotional resources on fighting your own internal states, those resources become available for everything else.

Putting It Into Practice

The ideas in this chapter aren't just conceptual. They point directly to specific things you can start doing differently, starting today. The goal isn't to overhaul everything at once. The goal is to make a few targeted transformations that begin moving you from symptom management toward transcendent engagement.

The first thing to do is audit your current management strategies. Take a piece of paper and write down the main ways you currently handle difficult internal experiences. Be honest. Do you scroll your phone when anxiety rises? Do you avoid certain conversations because they feel too charged? Do you procrastinate on important work when self-doubt shows up? Do you cancel plans when your mood dips? None of these things make you weak or flawed. They're extremely common. But they're worth seeing clearly. Once you can name your avoidance patterns, you can start making conscious choices about them instead of just running them automatically.

The second practice is the "sky and clouds" visualization, and it's worth doing once a day for the first week you work with this material. Sit somewhere quiet for three to five minutes. Close your eyes and picture a wide open sky. Now imagine your thoughts and feelings as clouds moving across that sky. Some clouds are dark and heavy. Some are light and wispy. They come and go. The sky itself doesn't change. It doesn't become the clouds. It simply holds them.

Now recognize that you are the sky in this picture, not the clouds. Your thoughts and feelings are passing through your awareness. They're not you. They don't define you. They don't have to determine what you do next. This visualization won't solve everything, but it does something specific and useful: it begins to create the experiential sense of distance between you and your mental content that defusion is built on.

The third practice is a daily values check-in. At the start of each day, before you look at your phone or begin your tasks, write down one value that matters to you and one specific action that would express that value today. Keep it small and concrete. The point isn't the size of the action. The point is the deliberate connection between a value and a behavior, made consciously, before the day's emotional weather has a chance to set your agenda for you.

The fourth practice is what you might call the "notice and name" technique for difficult moments. When you feel a difficult emotion rising, pause for just a few seconds and do two things. First, name the feeling: "I'm feeling anxious right now." Second, name it as a thought or sensation rather than a fact: "I'm having the feeling of anxiety" rather than "I am anxious." This small linguistic transformation does something real. It creates the tiny gap between you and the experience that defusion requires. You're not denying the feeling. You're not suppressing it. You're just changing your relationship to it.

These four practices build on each other. The audit shows you where you've been. The sky visualization begins building the experiential sense of self-as-observer. The values check-in points your day toward what matters rather than what's most comfortable. The notice-and-name technique gives you a real-time tool for the moments when difficult feelings show up and threaten to take over your decision-making. Together, they represent the beginning of a genuine transformation, not from feeling bad to feeling good but from being managed by your emotional state to being guided by your values.

The goal of this chapter was to show you clearly why the management approach has limits, what a better goal looks like, and what the mechanism is that makes that better goal achievable. Symptom reduction isn't the enemy. It's just not the finish line. The finish line is a life where your deepest values drive your choices, where difficult internal experiences are things you can hold without being controlled by them, and where your execution stays consistent even when your emotional weather is anything but calm. That's what transcendent functioning actually means. And the chapters ahead will show you exactly how to build it.

Chapter Three

Cognitive Defusion: Unhooking from the Mind

Your mind is incredibly good at one thing: generating thoughts. It produces them constantly, automatically, without asking your permission. Some of those thoughts are useful. Many aren't. And a significant number of them are the kind that, if you listen too closely, will quietly steer your life in a direction you never actually chose.

The problem isn't that you have difficult thoughts. Everyone does. The problem is what happens when you treat every thought as if it's a direct report on reality. When the thought "I'm going to mess this up" arrives before an important meeting, and you experience it as a fact rather than a mental event, your behavior follows the thought. You hesitate. You hold back. You prepare a hundred exit strategies instead of showing up fully. The thought didn't describe my reality. It created it.

That's what cognitive fusion looks like in

practice. And most people are doing it all day long without realizing it.

This chapter is about breaking that pattern. Not by silencing your thoughts, which isn't possible, but by changing your relationship to them so completely that they stop having automatic authority over what you do. The process is called cognitive defusion, and it's one of the most practical and well-supported tools in modern psychology. Once you understand it and start using it, you'll never think about your own thinking the same way again.

The Illusion of Thought-as-Fact

There's a default assumption most people carry without ever examining it. The assumption is this: if I'm thinking it, it must be true, or at least worth taking seriously as a real threat. This assumption runs so deep that most people don't even know it's there. It just operates in the background, turning every anxious thought into a potential emergency and every self-critical narrative into a verdict on who you are.

Psychologists call this cognitive fusion. You're

fused with a thought when you can't separate yourself from it. When "I'm not good enough" doesn't feel like a thought your mind produced, it feels like a fact about you. When "this is going to go wrong" doesn't feel like a prediction, it feels like a certainty. The thought and your experience of reality become one and the same thing. And once that happens, the thought doesn't just describe your situation. It controls your response to it.

Think about how this shows up in everyday life. A writer sits down to work, and the thought arrives: "Nothing I produce is original." If she's fused with that thought, she doesn't write. She stares at the screen, feels the weight of the thought as if it were a proven fact, and eventually closes the laptop. The thought was never verified. It was never tested against reality. It was simply believed, automatically, and her behavior followed. The thought had the power of a command, and she obeyed it without realizing she had a choice.

The "what if" spiral is one of the most common forms of fusion. "What if I say the wrong thing?" "What if this doesn't work out?" "What if they think less of me?" Each question feels urgent because your mind presents it as a genuine threat assessment rather than a hypothetical. Your nervous system can't tell the difference between a real danger and a vividly imagined one. So when you fuse with a "what if" thought, your body responds as if the feared outcome is already happening. Your heart rate rises. Your focus narrows. Your decision-making transformations toward protection rather than engagement are because you're not responding to what's actually in front of you. You're responding to a story your mind built.

This is where a lot of inconsistency comes from. The ambitious person who keeps stopping short isn't lacking talent or desire. They're fused with thoughts that keep presenting forward movement as dangerous. The entrepreneur who can't follow through isn't lazy. They're fused with thoughts that reframe every setback as evidence of permanent failure. The student who freezes before exams isn't unprepared. They're fused with thoughts that turn normal pre-test nerves into a forecast of catastrophe. In each case, the thought isn't the problem. The fusion is.

What makes fusion so messed up is that it feels like clarity. When you're fused with a thought, it doesn't feel like you're caught in a mental trap. It feels like you're seeing things accurately. The thought "I'm not ready for this" arrives with the weight of obvious truth. Of course you're not ready. Look at all the reasons. The mind is extremely good at building a case for whatever it believes, and when you're fused, you experience that case as airtight. You don't question the thought. You live inside it.

Consider a hypothetical scenario: someone like Daniel, a 31-year-old software developer who's been trying to launch a side project for two years. Daniel is technically skilled, genuinely motivated, and has a clear idea he believes in. But every time he gets close to showing his work to others, a cluster of thoughts arrives. "It's not perfect enough." "People will see the gaps in my knowledge." "Someone else has probably already done this better."

Daniel doesn't recognize these as thoughts. He experiences them as accurate assessments of the situation. So he keeps refining, keeps delaying, keeps waiting for a level of readiness that never quite arrives. The project has sat at ninety percent complete for months. Daniel isn't being held back by the quality of his work. He's being held back by his relationship to his own thinking.

The first step in changing that relationship is recognizing it for what it is. Not every thought that feels true is true. Not every thought that feels urgent is worth obeying. Your mind generates thoughts the way your lungs generate breath: automatically, constantly, without consulting you. Some of those thoughts are useful signals. Many are simply the mind doing what minds do: pattern-matching, threat-scanning, and running old narratives on repeat. The thought is a mental event. It's not a command. And the moment you can actually feel that distinction, rather than just understand it intellectually, something transforms or changes.

Reactive functioning, as described in the TFM model, is what happens when thoughts run the show. You feel anxious, so you avoid. You think "I'll fail," so you don't try. The internal state becomes the decision-maker. Defusion is what starts moving you out of that reactive mode. It creates the gap between stimulus and response that Viktor Frankl wrote about, the space where your freedom actually lives. You can't choose which thoughts arise. You absolutely can choose what you do with them.

The goal isn't to stop having difficult thoughts. That's not achievable, and chasing it only makes things worse. Research on thought suppression, going back to Daniel Wegner's work at Harvard in the 1980s, consistently shows that trying to push a thought out of your mind tends to make it more persistent, not less.

The more you tell yourself not to think about something, the more mental space it occupies. This is why traditional symptom management can backfire. When the goal is to eliminate the anxious thought, the anxious thought becomes the thing your mind is most focused on. You end up amplifying the very thing you were trying to quiet.

Defusion takes a completely different approach. Instead of fighting the thought, you change your stance toward it. You stop treating it as a fact that demands a response and start seeing it as a mental event you can observe. That transformation doesn't require the thought to disappear. It just requires you to stop being controlled by it. And that, it turns out, is enough to change everything.

Techniques for Mental Distance

Understanding cognitive fusion is one thing. Actually unhooking from your thoughts in real moments, when the anxiety is spiking and the self-doubt is loud, is something else entirely. That's where specific techniques come in. These aren't abstract concepts to think about. They're practical tools you can use immediately, and they work by doing something very specific: creating psychological distance between you and the thought.

Distance is the key word here. When you're fused with a thought, you're inside it. There's no space between you and the content. Defusion techniques create that space. They transform you from being the thought to observing the thought. And that transformation, even when it's small, changes what's possible next.

The most direct technique is *labeling*. When a difficult thought arrives, instead of experiencing it as a fact, you name it as a thought. The phrase is simple: "I'm having the thought that..." So instead of "I'm going to fail this presentation," you say to yourself, "I'm having the thought that I'm going to fail this presentation." Instead of "Nobody respects me," you say, "I'm having the thought that nobody respects me." This sounds almost too simple to matter. It isn't.

What the labeling technique does is reframe the thought from a direct statement about reality to a description of a mental event. "I'm going to fail" presents itself as a fact. "I'm having the thought that I'm going to fail" makes visible the fact that a mind produced this, that it's one mental event among thousands your brain will generate today, and that you don't have to treat it as ground truth. The content of the thought hasn't changed. Your relationship to it has. And your relationship to it is what determines your behavior.

You can extend this even further. Some people find it useful to add one more layer: "I notice that I'm having the thought that..." This creates even more distance. You're now the observer of the observer, watching yourself have a thought rather than being inside it. Try it right now with whatever thought has been most persistent for you lately. Say the full phrase in your head: "I notice that I'm having the thought that..." and fill in the blank. Notice what happens to the weight of that thought. For most people, it lightens even slightly. That lightening is the beginning of diffusion.

The second technique is the *"leaves on a stream" visualization*, which comes directly from Acceptance and Commitment Therapy and has been used in clinical settings for decades. Here's exactly how to do it. Find a quiet place where you won't be interrupted for five to ten minutes. Close your eyes and picture yourself sitting beside a slow-moving stream. The water is clear and calm. Leaves float on the surface, drifting past you at an easy pace. Now, as each thought arises in your mind, place it on a leaf. It doesn't matter what the thought is. A worry, a plan, a memory, a judgment, a random image. Whatever appears, put it on a leaf and watch it float downstream. You're not trying to speed up the stream. You're not trying to stop the leaves. You're simply watching them pass.

If you notice yourself getting pulled into a thought and following it downstream instead of watching it go, that's fine. It's going to happen. When you notice it, gently come back to the bank and resume watching. The act of returning is itself the practice. Every time you catch yourself fused with a thought and choose to step back to the observer position, you're strengthening the exact mental muscle that defusion requires.

Do this exercise once a day for two weeks. Not occasionally. Daily. The reason is that defusion, like any skill, builds through repetition. The first few times, it might feel forced or artificial. That's normal. By the end of two weeks, most people report that the sense of being an observer of their thoughts rather than a prisoner of them starts to feel more natural. The stream visualization works because it gives your mind a concrete structure for a process that's otherwise abstract. Instead of trying to "think differently about your thoughts," you're doing something specific and sensory that your brain can actually practice.

The third technique is the *whiteboard visualization*, and it's particularly useful for recurring negative thoughts, the ones that show up again and again with the same content. Here's how it works. Picture a large whiteboard. On it, write the thought that keeps returning. See it clearly in your mind. Now step back from the whiteboard. Notice that you're the person standing in the room, looking at the whiteboard. The words are on the board. They're not inside you. They're not you. They're marks on a surface. Now pick up an eraser and wipe the board clean. The thought is gone. The board is blank. Now notice that the thought will probably come back. When it does, write it on the board again. Erase it again. You're not trying to destroy the thought permanently. You're practicing the physical and visual experience of separating yourself from it, of being the person who holds the eraser rather than the person who is the writing.

This technique is especially effective for the inner critic. The voice that says you're not capable, not ready, not worthy. When you can see those words on a whiteboard instead of experiencing them as internal truth, they lose their authority. You can read them, acknowledge that your mind produced them, and choose not to let them direct your next action.

The fourth technique is what's sometimes called *"thanking the mind."* This one can feel strange at first, but it's grounded in a real principle. When a difficult thought arrives, instead of arguing with it or trying to push it away, you simply say, "Thanks, mind." "Thanks for that warning." "Thanks for the reminder." This isn't sarcasm. It's a genuine acknowledgment that your mind is trying to protect you, even when its methods are unhelpful. The mind generates threat-focused thoughts because that's part of its evolutionary design. It's doing its job. Thanking it for the thought, rather than fighting it, removes the adversarial quality from the interaction. You're no longer at war with your own mind. You're just noticing what it's doing, acknowledging it, and choosing your response independently.

A specific version of this: when you notice a self-critical thought, say out loud or in your head, "Thanks, mind. I've got it from here." Then take the action you were going to take anyway. The thought doesn't need to be resolved or disproven before you move. You just need to not be controlled by it. "Thanks, mind. I've got it from here" is a practical way to signal that you've received the thought's input and you're making the call yourself.

These techniques work because they all do the same fundamental thing: they transform you from being inside the thought to being outside it. They move you from reactive functioning, where the thought dictates your behavior, to a position where you can observe the thought, acknowledge it, and then choose your response based on what you actually value rather than what the thought is demanding.

It's worth being honest about what defusion doesn't do. It doesn't make difficult thoughts disappear. It doesn't make uncomfortable feelings go away. It doesn't guarantee that the inner critic will quiet down or that the "what if" spiral will stop generating scenarios. What it does is remove those thoughts and feelings from the driver's seat. They can still be in the car. They just don't get to choose the destination. That's the distinction between regulated functioning, where you're managing your thoughts, and the beginning of transcendent functioning, where your thoughts are present but no longer in charge.

The more you practice these techniques, the more automatic the observer stance becomes. You start catching fusion earlier. You notice when a thought is pulling you in and you have a moment to choose. That moment is small. But it's everything. It's the difference between a life that's shaped by your values and a life that's shaped by whatever your mind happens to be afraid of on any given day.

Your Practice Plan: What to Do Starting Today

Understanding defusion intellectually is a starting point. The real transformation happens through consistent, specific practice. The following steps are designed to be done in sequence over the next two weeks. Each one builds on the last, and together they create the foundation for a genuinely different relationship with your own thinking.

Step 1: Identify your three most recurring negative thoughts. Take ten minutes today with a pen and paper. Write down the three thoughts that show up most often and cause the most disruption. Be specific. Not "I worry a lot" but "I keep having the thought that I'm falling behind everyone else my age." Not "I'm self-critical" but "I keep having the thought that I'm not as capable as people think I am." Getting specific matters because vague patterns are hard to work with. Concrete, named thoughts are something you can actually practice defusing. Once you have your three, write them at the top of a page and keep that page somewhere visible for the next two weeks.

Step 2: Practice the labeling technique with those three thoughts every day. Each morning, read your three thoughts from the page. For each one, say the full phrase out loud: "I'm having the thought that..." and read the thought. Do this slowly. Don't rush it. The goal is to feel the difference between the thought as a fact and the thought as a mental event. This takes about two minutes. Do it before you check your phone, before you start your day, before the noise of the morning takes over. Two minutes, every morning, for fourteen days. That's it. This single practice, done consistently, starts to rewire how automatically you fuse with those particular thoughts.

Step 3: Run the leaves on a stream exercise five times this week. Not every day this week, but five times. Pick five days, block ten minutes, and do the full visualization as described earlier in this chapter. After each session, write one sentence in a notebook: What thought came up most persistently, and what did it feel like to watch it float away rather than follow it? The writing isn't for analysis. It's for anchoring the experience. When you write down what you noticed, you're reinforcing the observer position in a way that carries over into the rest of your day.

Step 4: Use the whiteboard visualization for your single most disruptive thought. From your list of three, pick the one that causes the most interference with your actual goals. Maybe it's the one that stops you from starting important work. Maybe it's the one that makes you pull back in conversations. Whatever it is, run the whiteboard visualization with that specific thought once a day for a week. Write it on the imagined board. Step back. Erase it. Repeat when it returns. Do this for seven consecutive days. By day seven, most people notice that the thought still arrives but carries less automatic weight. You've practiced, repeatedly and specifically, the experience of being separate from them. That practice changes your default response.

Step 5: Apply "thanks, mind" in real time. Starting today, whenever one of your three recurring thoughts shows up during your actual day, use the phrase. Out loud if you're alone. Silently if you're not. "Thanks, mind. I've got it from here. "Then do the next thing you were going to do anyway. Don't wait until the thought feels resolved. Don't wait until you feel ready. Do the next thing while the thought is still present. This is the step that moves defusion from a practice exercise into a lived skill. You're not just doing it in quiet meditation. You're doing it in the middle of your real life, which is exactly where it needs to work.

These five steps aren't complicated. But they require consistency, and consistency is the one thing that separates people who understand defusion from people who actually develop it as a functional skill. The techniques only work if you use them. And you'll only use them if you've built the habit of using them before the difficult moments arrive.

One more thing worth saying clearly. There will be days when you're so fused with a thought that none of these techniques feel accessible. The anxiety is too loud. The self-doubt is too insistent. The thought feels too real to step back from. That's going to happen, and it doesn't mean the practice isn't working. It means you're human. When that happens, the only move is to name it: "I'm really confused by this right now." That's it. Just naming the fusion, without trying to fix it in that moment, is itself a small act of defusion. You've stepped back just enough to observe that you're stuck. And that tiny observation is the beginning of getting unstuck.

The capacity to operate above your emotional state doesn't come from having fewer difficult thoughts. It comes from building a stable, practiced relationship with your thoughts where you are the observer, not the observed. Where you are the one holding the eraser, not the one who is writing on the board. Every time you practice that relationship, you're building the internal structure that makes consistent, value-driven functioning possible regardless of what your mind happens to be generating on any given day.

That structure is what the rest of this book continues to build. Defusion is the first pillar. It creates the space. What you do with that space is what the next chapters are about.

Chapter Four

Experiential Expansion: Welcoming the Storm

You've learned to create distance from your thoughts. That's the work of diffusion, and if you've been practicing it, you've already started to notice something important: the thought isn't the problem. The relationship to the thought is. The same principle applies to something even more visceral than thought. It applies to the raw physical experience of difficult emotions themselves.

Thoughts are words and images. Emotions are something else entirely. They live in your body. The tight chest before a hard conversation. The sick feeling in your stomach when something goes wrong. The restless, electric tension of anxiety that makes it almost impossible to sit still, and these aren't abstract mental events; they're physical experiences and can be overwhelming in a way that thoughts rarely are. You can sometimes talk yourself out of a thought. You can't always talk yourself out of a feeling that's firing through your nervous system at full intensity.

Most people respond to intense emotional discomfort the same way they respond to physical pain. They try to make it stop. They distract themselves, numb out, avoid the situation that triggered it, or push the feeling down as hard as they can. And for a while, those strategies seemed to work. The discomfort fades. The pressure eases. You feel better, at least temporarily. The problem is what happens over time. Every time you successfully escape a difficult feeling, your brain logs that escape as a victory.

The message it receives is that feeling was dangerous, and getting away from it was the right move. So the next time that feeling shows up, your brain treats it with even more urgency. The avoidance response gets stronger. The feeling itself becomes more threatening. You haven't solved anything. You've trained yourself to be more afraid of your own emotional experience than you were before. This is the cycle that keeps people stuck at the regulated level of functioning, managing their discomfort just well enough to survive, but never developing the capacity to actually move through it.

This chapter is about breaking that cycle. Not by toughening up or forcing yourself to feel bad on purpose, but by developing a fundamentally different relationship with your inner experience. One where difficult emotions are no longer emergencies to escape but signals to observe. One where the storm inside you becomes something you can hold, steady and clear, without being swept away by it.

Turning Toward Discomfort

There's a term in psychology called *experiential avoidance*. It describes the habit of organizing your behavior around escaping or minimizing uncomfortable internal experiences: thoughts, feelings, physical sensations, and memories. If it's unpleasant, the avoidance response says, "Get away from it." And the more you follow that response, the more your life shrinks around the things you're willing to feel.

Experiential avoidance is one of the most well-studied predictors of psychological suffering. Research consistently shows that people who score high on experiential avoidance report lower quality of life, more anxiety and depression, less satisfaction in relationships, and worse performance across almost every domain. The connection isn’t subtle. The more you try to avoid your own inner experience, the worse things tend to get—not because the feelings themselves are so destructive, but because the avoidance strategy consumes enormous amounts of energy and keeps you from engaging fully with your actual life.

Think about how much mental bandwidth goes into avoidance. You scan for situations that might trigger anxiety and pre-emptively avoid them. You monitor your internal state constantly, watching for signs that something uncomfortable is rising. You maintain a whole set of behaviors, scrolling, snacking, staying busy, and keeping the TV on, that exist primarily to prevent you from having to sit with your own experience. All of that takes energy. Energy that could be going somewhere useful. When you add it up across a day, across a week, it's staggering how much of your cognitive and emotional capacity is being spent on running from yourself!

And the cruel part is that it doesn't even work. Not really. Avoiding a feeling doesn't dissolve it. It just delays it and often amplifies it. The anxiety you didn't let yourself feel before the meeting shows up during it. The grief kept you busy avoiding sleep at 2am, when there was nothing left to distract you. The frustration you swallowed in the moment comes out sideways in a conversation that had nothing to do with the original source. Suppressed emotional experience doesn't disappear. It goes underground and waits.

There's a second layer of suffering that avoidance creates, and it's worth understanding clearly. Psychologists sometimes refer to this as a secondary layer of suffering, where the primary discomfort—anxiety, sadness, or frustration—is compounded by reactions to that discomfort itself.

The primary suffering is the original discomfort. The secondary suffering is everything you feel about that discomfort—the anxiety about the anxiety, the shame about feeling sad, the frustration about feeling frustrated. The thought that says, "I shouldn't be feeling this" or "What's wrong with me that I can't handle this?"

Secondary suffering is often more intense than the original feeling, and it is largely driven by resistance to the initial experience. When you stop fighting the primary experience, the secondary layer often begins to diminish on its own.

Consider a hypothetical scenario: someone like

Aisha, a 32-year-old project manager who describes herself as someone who "doesn't do feelings well." She's high-functioning at work, organized, efficient, and well-liked. But whenever a situation triggers real emotional discomfort, whether it's conflict with a colleague, feedback that stings, or the low-grade anxiety she feels before important presentations, her default is to push it down and power through. She tells herself she doesn't have time to feel things. She'll deal with it later. Later never really comes. What she's noticed over time is that the pushing-down takes more and more effort. She's increasingly exhausted by mid-week. She finds herself snapping at people she cares about. She's starting to feel numb in situations that used to excite her. The avoidance is working in the sense that she's still functioning. But it's costing her in ways she can't quite name. The energy she's using to hold the lid on her emotional experience is energy that's no longer available for anything else.

Aisha's situation is extremely common. The high-achiever who treats emotional experience as an obstacle to efficiency. The person who's learned to be so good at suppressing discomfort that they've also suppressed a significant portion of their aliveness.

Turning toward discomfort means something specific. It means choosing, deliberately and consciously, to allow a difficult feeling to be present rather than immediately trying to make it stop. It doesn't mean wallowing in it. It doesn't mean dramatizing it or letting it run your behavior. It means treating the feeling as something you can observe rather than something you must escape. You turn toward it the way you'd turn toward an unfamiliar sound in the dark. Not to be consumed by it, but to see it clearly.

When you do this, something often surprising happens. The feeling doesn't grow the way you expected. In fact, when you stop fighting an emotional experience, it frequently peaks and then begins to subside on its own. Emotions are designed to move. The word "emotion" shares its root with the word "motion." Feelings are energy in motion through your body. They're meant to arise, be felt, and pass. What keeps them stuck, what turns a temporary wave into a permanent flood, is the resistance—the fighting and the frantic effort to escape. When you remove the resistance, the feeling often moves through faster than you thought it would.

That insight is worth sitting with. The thing

you've been spending enormous energy trying to avoid often passes more quickly when you stop avoiding it. The anxiety before a difficult conversation typically peaks in the minutes before the conversation starts. If you let yourself feel it rather than fight it, it tends to drop significantly once the conversation begins. The dread of a task is almost always worse than the task itself. The anticipatory suffering, fueled by avoidance, is the real cost. The actual feeling, when you let yourself have it, is usually more manageable than you feared.

Turning toward discomfort is an active choice, not a passive one. It takes more courage than avoidance does, at least initially. Avoidance feels like protection. Turning toward it feels like risk. But over time, the math reverses. Avoidance is the strategy with compounding costs. Turning toward it is the strategy with compounding returns. Every time you let yourself feel something difficult without fleeing it, you build evidence that you can handle it. Your window of emotional tolerance expands. The next difficult feeling arrives, and you meet it with a little more steadiness than before. That steadiness, built through repeated practice, is the foundation of transcendent functioning. Urge Surfing and Somatic Awareness

Knowing that you should turn toward discomfort and actually doing it when the discomfort is intense are two very different things. Abstract understanding doesn't help much when your heart is racing, your chest is tight, and every signal in your body is screaming that something is wrong. What you need in those moments is a concrete, specific technique. Something you can actually do with your hands, your breath, and your attention.

That's where somatic awareness comes in. Somatic means relating to the body. Somatic: That's where somatic awareness comes in. Somatic means relating to the body. Somatic awareness is the practice of paying deliberate, detailed attention to the physical sensations in your body without immediately reacting to them. It's the skill of noticing what's actually happening at the level of physical experience, separate from the story your mind is building around that experience.

Here's how to practice this in a moment of real emotional intensity. When you notice a difficult feeling rising, instead of immediately trying to manage it or escape it, transform your attention to the physical sensations in your body. Get specific. Where exactly do you feel it? Is it in your chest, your throat, your stomach, your shoulders? What does it feel like physically? Is it tight or loose? Hot or cold? Sharp or dull? Is it moving or staying in one place? Does it have a texture, a weight, a size?

These questions sound unusual, but they do something precise: they move your attention from the narrative layer of the experience to the sensory layer. And at the sensory layer, the experience is almost always more manageable than the story about it suggested.

You're not trying to make the sensation go away. You're simply observing it with curiosity, the way a scientist might examine something unfamiliar. What happens when you bring this kind of careful, non-judgmental attention to a physical sensation is often remarkable. The sensation changes. It transforms, moves, softens, or intensifies briefly before subsiding. When you observe it without resistance, you stop adding the fuel of avoidance to it. You let it be what it is, which is energy moving through your body, and you watch what it does when it's allowed to move.

Urge surfing is a specific application of this principle, and it's one of the most powerful tools in this entire chapter. The technique was developed in the context of addiction treatment, specifically to help people ride out intense cravings without acting on them (Marlatt & Gordon, 1985). But its application is much broader than addiction.

Any intense impulse—the urge to snap at someone when you're frustrated, to check your phone compulsively when you're anxious, to abandon a difficult task when it gets uncomfortable, or to eat when you're stressed rather than hungry—can be worked with through urge surfing.

The core insight behind urge surfing is this: every urge has a physical shape. It builds, peaks, and subsides, like a wave. If you can observe that wave without acting on it, you discover something important. The urge doesn't keep building forever. It reaches a peak, and then it drops. You don't have to ride it out for long. You just have to ride it out past the peak. And each time you do, the wave gets a little less powerful the next time it comes.

Here's the specific practice. When you notice an intense urge or impulse arising, do these four things in sequence. First, name it: "I'm noticing an urge to [specific behavior]." Second, locate it in your body: where do you feel this urge physically?

Third, describe its qualities: how intense is it on a scale of one to ten? What does it feel like physically? Is it building or already at its peak? Fourth, watch it: keep your attention on the physical sensation and observe what it does over the next two to five minutes without acting on it. Breathe normally. Don't fight the sensation. Don't try to speed it up or slow it down. Just watch.

Most people find that by the time they've completed these four steps, the urge has already begun to subside. Not because they suppressed it, but because they observed it. The act of careful, curious observation changes your relationship to the urge from one of being controlled by it to one of watching it. And from the observer position, you have a choice. You can choose to act on the urge, or you can choose to let the wave pass and then decide what to do next based on what you actually value rather than what the impulse was demanding.

Practice urge surfing on small, low-stakes impulses first. The urge to check your phone when you're in the middle of focused work. The urge to get up and make a snack when you're sitting with a task that feels hard. The urge to send a message immediately when you're feeling anxious about a relationship. These small urges are a perfect training ground because the stakes are low enough that you can practice without the pressure of a high-intensity situation. Every time you successfully surf a small urge, you're building the same skill you'll use when the bigger waves come.

Somatic awareness and urge surfing together give you something that purely cognitive techniques can't: a way to work with your body rather than against it. Your nervous system is not your enemy. It's doing exactly what it was designed to do. When you develop the ability to observe its signals with curiosity instead of fear, you stop being at war with your own physiology. You start to trust that you can feel intense things and still choose your response. That trust is not a small thing. It's the ground on which consistent, value-driven behavior is built.

The Power of Mindful Allowance

There's a concept in mindfulness practice often referred to as the observing self. It's the part of you that notices your experience without being consumed by it—the part that can watch a thought arise and pass, feel an emotion without becoming the emotion, and remain steady even when everything inside you is moving.

You've had access to the observing self your whole life. You've experienced it in moments of unexpected calm during chaos... Those moments weren't accidents. They were glimpses of a capacity that can be developed deliberately.

Mindful allowance is the practice of accessing that observing self on purpose, even when—especially when—your internal experience is intense. It's different from passive resignation, and that distinction is critical. Passive resignation says, "I give up..." Mindful allowance says something entirely different. It says, "I see what's here." "I'm not going to fight it. I'm going to let it be present while I remain present too."

The difference is agency. Passive resignation removes you from the equation. Mindful allowance keeps you fully in it. You're not surrendering to the storm. You're choosing to stand in it without running. That choice, made deliberately, is an act of courage, not weakness.

Here's a concrete way to understand the distinction. Suppose you're sitting with a wave of anxiety about something important coming up. Passive resignation sounds like "I'm anxious, there's nothing I can do, I just have to wait for this to pass." "Mindful allowance" sounds like "I'm noticing anxiety right now. I can feel it in my chest and shoulders. I'm going to let it be here without trying to push it away. I'm still the one choosing what I do next." One is being swept away. The other is standing in the current with your feet on the ground.

The mindfulness tradition offers a useful image for this. *Think of yourself as the sky*. Your thoughts, feelings, and sensations are the weather. The weather changes constantly. Storms come. Sunshine comes. Clouds gather and disperse. But the sky doesn't become the weather. The sky holds the weather. No matter how severe the storm, the sky remains. You are the sky. Your difficult emotions are weather passing through you, not the truth of who you are.

Developing the observing self isn't a passive process. It requires practice, and the most direct practice is a structured body scan (Kabat-Zinn, 2003). Here's exactly how to do it when you're stressed or overwhelmed. Set a timer for five minutes. Sit comfortably with your feet on the floor and your hands resting in your lap. Close your eyes. Start at the top of your head and slowly move your attention downward through your body. Scalp, forehead, jaw, neck, shoulders, chest, stomach, lower back, hips, thighs, knees, calves, feet. At each area, pause for a few seconds and simply notice what's there. Tension, warmth, tightness, numbness, ease. *Don't try to change anything.* Don't try to relax anything. Just notice and move on.

When you reach your feet, pause for a moment and then slowly bring your attention back upward. By the time you've completed one full scan, five minutes will have passed. You will almost certainly feel different than you did when you started. Not because you fixed anything, but because you spent five minutes in the observer position, watching your physical experience with curiosity rather than reacting to it with alarm. The nervous system responds to this kind of attention. It begins to down-regulate, not because you forced it to, but because you stopped adding the fuel of resistance and fear to it.

Do this body scan every time you notice significant stress or emotional intensity. Not occasionally. *Every time.* Make it the first response rather than the last resort. Most people reach for distraction, food, their phone, or a coping technique when stress rises. The body scan asks you to do something counterintuitive: to turn toward the experience first, observe it fully, and then decide what to do next. That sequence, turning toward, observing, then choosing, is the practical structure of mindful allowance.

There's a subtlety here that's worth naming. Mindful allowance doesn't mean you stay in a difficult emotional state indefinitely. It doesn't mean you never seek support, never take action, or never make changes to situations that are genuinely harmful. Allowance is about your relationship to the internal experience, *not about tolerating* external circumstances that need to change. You can fully feel your anger about an unfair situation and still take decisive action to address it. In fact, when you're not spending energy fighting the feeling of anger, you often think more clearly about what action actually makes sense. The feeling and the action are separate things. Allowance handles the feeling. Your values handle the action.

One more practice worth building into your daily routine. At the end of each day, take two minutes to sit quietly and ask yourself one question: What did I allow today that I would normally have avoided? It doesn't have to be dramatic. Maybe you let yourself feel disappointed about something without immediately reframing it. Maybe you sat with uncertainty about a decision instead of rushing to resolve it. Maybe you felt the discomfort of a difficult conversation rather than numbing out afterward. Whatever it was, name it. Write it down if you can. This brief daily reflection does something specific: it trains your attention to notice the moments when you chose allowance over avoidance. And what you notice, you reinforce. Over time, allowance becomes less effortful because you've been systematically building awareness of it as a real, available choice.

The deeper transformation that all of this creates is a change in your relationship to your own internal world. You stop experiencing your emotions as threats that need to be managed and start experiencing them as information that can be observed. You stop treating discomfort as evidence that something has gone wrong and start treating it as a normal feature of an engaged life. You stop waiting to feel ready or calm or confident before you act and start acting from your values while the difficult feelings are still present. That transformation is not a small adjustment to your existing way of operating. It's a fundamental restructuring of how you process your own experience. And it's exactly what operating above your emotions actually requires.

What You Take Forward

Everything in this chapter points toward one central capacity: the ability to hold your inner experience without being held hostage by it. That capacity is built through practice, not insight. Reading this chapter is a start. What happens in the next two weeks determines whether these ideas become skills or stay as concepts.

Here are your specific practices, built from everything covered in this chapter.

Practice one: The five-minute body scan is done every time stress or emotional intensity rises. Not once a week. Not when you remember. Every time. Set the timer, close your eyes, and move your attention from the top of your head to your feet, noticing without changing. This is your primary tool for accessing the observer position in real time. The more consistently you use it, the more automatic the transformation to an observer stance becomes.

Practice two: Urge surfing for minor daily impulses, starting today. Pick one recurring small impulse: the phone check, the stress snack, or the urge to close the difficult email without responding. When it arises, name it, locate it in your body, describe its physical qualities, and watch it for two to three minutes without acting on it. Do this with the same small impulse every day for one week. By day seven, you'll have direct experiential evidence that you can feel an urge at full intensity and still choose your behavior. That evidence is more valuable than any amount of theoretical understanding.

Practice three: The daily two-minute allowance reflection. Each evening, write down one thing you allowed today that you'd normally have avoided. Keep it specific. "I felt the anxiety about the deadline instead of distracting myself" is useful. But "I was being more mindful today" is too vague to build anything on. Specificity is what makes this reflection a genuine practice rather than a ritual.

Practice four: The "turn toward" pause in

moments of avoidance. Whenever you notice yourself reaching for a distraction or avoidance behavior, pause for ten seconds before you act on it. In those ten seconds, ask, "What am I trying not to feel right now?" Name the feeling. Locate it in your body. Then decide whether to proceed with the distraction or to stay with the feeling for a few more minutes. You're not banning distraction. You're inserting a moment of conscious choice between the impulse and the behavior. That moment is where your freedom lives.

These four practices work together. The body scan builds your observer capacity. Urge surfing builds your tolerance for intense impulses. The daily reflection builds your awareness of allowance as a real choice. The turn-toward pause builds the habit of conscious response over automatic reaction. Together, they expand your window of emotional tolerance in a way that carries directly into every area where you've been inconsistent, every place where difficult feelings have been quietly running the show.

The goal was never to stop feeling. The goal is to feel fully and still choose wisely. That's what this chapter has been building toward, and it's what the practices above will start to make real in your daily life.

Chapter Five

Attachment Reduction: Loosening the Grip

There's a particular kind of suffering that doesn't come from what's happening to you. It comes from how tightly you're holding on to how you think things should be. You've probably felt it. The rigid certainty that you need to feel confident before you can act. The quiet insistence that this plan has to work out exactly as you imagined. The deep, almost unconscious belief that you are a specific kind of person and that anything threatening that identity is a problem to be solved. None of these things announce themselves as attachments. They feel like common sense. They feel like standards. They feel like you.

That's what makes them so hard to see.

Cognitive defusion, which you worked through in Chapter 2, helps you step back from the thoughts your mind generates. *Experiential expansion,* from Chapter 3, builds your capacity to hold difficult feelings without fleeing them. Both of those processes create space. But there's a more subtle layer underneath both of them, a layer that determines how much of that space you actually get to use. That layer is attachment. Specifically, the attachments you've formed to particular self-narratives, particular outcomes, and particular conditions that you've decided must be in place before you can function well (Hayes et al., 2006).

This chapter is about loosening those attachments. Not abandoning what matters to you, but releasing the grip that turns meaningful preferences into psychological chains.

The Suffering of Rigid Clinging

Think about holding a butterfly in your fist. If you squeeze tightly enough to be sure you won't lose it, you'll crush it. If you open your hand completely, it flies away. The only way to actually have it is to hold it loosely, with just enough presence to feel it without controlling it. Most people are walking around with their fists clenched around their own lives and wondering why everything feels so fragile.

Rigid attachment works the same way. When

you grip a desired outcome too tightly, the energy you spend protecting that outcome becomes its own source of suffering. You're not fully present to what's happening because you're too busy monitoring whether it's matching your expectations. You're not genuinely engaged because part of you is always braced for the moment things go wrong. The very act of holding on so hard prevents you from experiencing what you're trying to hold.

Psychologists who work in the ACT tradition describe this as experiential rigidity. It's the opposite of the psychological flexibility you've been building. Where flexibility allows you to move with your experience, rigidity locks you into a specific version of how things should be. And the more locked in you are, the more friction you generate every time reality doesn't cooperate, which, as you've probably noticed, is fairly often.

The attachments that create the most damage aren't usually the obvious ones. You probably already know that being obsessively attached to a single career outcome is risky or that demanding perfection from yourself is exhausting. Those are visible. The more dangerous attachments are the ones that feel completely reasonable. These feel like reasonable positions, not attachments. But when reality doesn't match them, and it frequently won't, the suffering is immediate and real.

There's also a category of attachment that's particularly relevant: the story you tell yourself about who you are, what you're capable of, and what kind of person you're supposed to be. These narratives can be positive or negative, and both kinds can trap you. The person who's attached to being "the capable one" suffers when they struggle. The person attached to the label "anxious person" uses that story to justify avoidance, even when they've grown well past the version of themselves that story describes.

Consider a hypothetical scenario: someone like Nadia, a 36-year-old product designer who built her professional identity around being the most prepared person in any room. She researches exhaustively before meetings. She never speaks up unless she's certain. She's built a reputation for thoroughness, and that reputation means a great deal to her. But lately, her industry is moving faster than her preparation can keep up with. Decisions get made in real time. Opinions are expected on the spot. And Nadia finds herself increasingly paralyzed, not because she lacks insight, but because the situation keeps threatening her attachment to being the prepared one. She can't contribute fluidly because contributing fluidly would require her to let go of the identity she's organized her professional life around. The attachment that once helped her succeed has become the ceiling that's keeping her stuck.

Nadia's situation isn't unusual. The self-narratives that served you at one stage of your life often become the very things that limit you at the next stage. And the tighter you hold them, the more they constrain what's possible.

The first step in loosening any attachment is identifying it clearly. Not in a vague, general way, but with specific language. An attachment isn't just "I care about doing well." It's "I believe that if I don't perform perfectly, it means something permanent and serious about who I am." "An attachment isn't just 'I want this project to succeed.' "I've decided that this project succeeding is the thing that will prove I'm capable, and if it doesn't, I won't know how to move forward. When you can stake the attachment that specifically, you can start to see it as a belief rather than a fact.

And beliefs, unlike facts, can be questioned.

Take ten minutes right now and write down your three most non-negotiable internal rules. The ones that, when violated, produce the strongest emotional reaction. "I should always be in control of my emotions." "I need people to respect my work." "I have to be consistent, or I'm failing." These are your attachments. They're not character flaws. They're stories that have calcified into requirements. And requirements, when unmet, produce suffering in exact proportion to how tightly you've been holding them.

De-centering the Self-Concept

You are not a fixed thing. You know this intellectually. But the way most people actually operate suggests they've forgotten it completely. The labels people carry, "I'm an introvert," "I'm not a morning person," "I'm the responsible one," and "I'm someone who struggles with confidence," function less like descriptions and more like job titles. They come with expectations, limitations, and a whole set of behaviors that feel required by the role. And the longer you hold a label, the more evidence your mind finds to confirm it and the less room you have to act outside it.

This is what psychologists call cognitive rigidity around the self-concept. Your self-concept is the collection of beliefs you hold about who you are. It's not inherently a problem. Having some sense of who you are gives you continuity and direction. The problem arises when that self-concept becomes so fixed that it stops being a useful map and starts being a cage. When "I'm not creative" stops being an observation and becomes a rule. When "I'm the responsible one in my family" stops being a role you chose and becomes an obligation you can't escape. When "I've always struggled with follow-through" stops being a historical pattern and becomes a prediction you unconsciously fulfill.

De-centering the self-concept doesn't mean abandoning your sense of self. It means holding it more lightly. It means recognizing that you are a multifaceted, context-dependent, constantly evolving human being, and that no single label, however accurate it felt at one point, captures the full reality of what you're capable of.

The ACT model introduces a concept called "self-as-context" that's useful here. The idea is that there's a version of you that exists behind all the labels, behind all the stories, behind all the roles. It's the part of you that notices all of those things—

the observer and the awareness that's present when you're anxious and also present when you're calm. Present when you succeed, and present when you fail. This observing self doesn't change based on what's happening. It's the stable ground beneath the transforming weather of your experience.

When you can access that part of yourself, you're no longer dependent on any particular label to feel grounded. You can hold the label "I'm someone who struggles with confidence" without being defined by it, because you know that the part of you doing the holding is bigger than the label itself.

Here's a specific practice for de-centering a label that's been limiting you. Start by identifying one label you carry that you suspect has been functioning as a constraint. Be specific. Not "I have low self-esteem" but "I carry the label of someone who isn't good at speaking up in groups." *Once you have it, do the following sequence over three days.*

On day one, write the label at the top of a page. Underneath it, write every piece of evidence your mind uses to support it. Be thorough. Let your mind make its full case. Don't argue with it yet. Just let it say everything it wants to say about why this label is accurate.

On day two, write the label again. This time, underneath it, write every piece of evidence that contradicts it. There were times you acted outside the label. Moments where the label didn't apply. Situations where you surprised yourself. Your mind will resist this. It's been building the case for the label for a long time, and it won't give it up easily. Write the contradictions anyway. You don't need many. Even two or three genuine examples are enough to begin cracking the absolute certainty the label carries.

On day three, write this sentence at the top of the page: "I sometimes have the experience of [label], and I'm also capable of [opposite behavior]." Read it out loud. Notice how it feels different from treating the label as a fixed identity. You're not denying your history. You're refusing to let your history be the only thing that's true about you. That refusal is the beginning of de-centering.

The reason this matters for your functioning is direct and practical. When your self-concept is rigid, your behavior is predictable in the worst way. You act in ways that confirm the label, not because the label is accurate, but because the label is what you expect of yourself. The student who's labeled themselves as "bad at exams" doesn't just perform poorly on exams, either. They study less, panic earlier, give up faster, and then point to the poor result as proof that the label was right all along. The label shapes the behavior, and the behavior confirms the label. Breaking that loop requires loosening your grip on the label itself, not just trying harder within it.

You are not the responsible one. You are not the anxious one. You are not the person who always struggles with X. You are a person who has had those experiences, and you are also capable of experiences that don't fit those descriptions. The difference between those two framings is the difference between a fixed ceiling and an open sky. One tells you what you are. The other reminds you that what you are is far more than any single story can hold.

Relinquishing Control Over Outcomes

Here's something worth sitting with honestly. A significant portion of your suffering probably has nothing to do with what's actually happening right now. It has to do with the gap between what's happening and what you decided should be happening. The project that isn't progressing at the pace you set for it. The relationship that isn't developing the way you imagined. The career that isn't unfolding according to the timeline you built in your head. The version of yourself that isn't as consistent, as disciplined, or as far along as you thought you'd be by now. *The suffering isn't in the reality. It's in the distance between the reality and the requirement.*

This is the hedonic treadmill, working against you in a specific way. You set an outcome. You invest your sense of well-being in that outcome. You work toward it. And even when progress is real and genuine, the treadmill keeps moving, and the sense of arrival never quite comes. Because the attachment isn't really to the outcome. It's about the feeling you believe the outcome will produce. The sense of finally being enough. Finally being safe. Finally being free from the uncertainty that's been following you. And since no external outcome can permanently produce those internal states, the treadmill keeps running and you keep chasing.

Relinquishing control over outcomes isn't resignation. It's not the same as not caring. You can pursue goals with full intensity and genuine investment while simultaneously releasing your grip on the specific form those goals must take. The distinction is between being driven by your values and being driven by your attachment to a predetermined result. Values are durable. They guide you through the unexpected turns, the failed attempts, the plans that don't survive contact with reality. Attachment to a specific outcome makes every deviation feel like failure, even when the deviation is actually taking you somewhere better.

Think about what it actually costs you to be tightly attached to a specific result. You spend mental energy monitoring whether you're on track. You feel anxious when variables outside your control transform. You make decisions based on protecting the outcome rather than responding intelligently to what's in front of you. You lose the ability to adapt, because adaptation requires being willing to let the original plan go. And you lose access to the satisfaction available in the process itself, because the process only has value insofar as it's leading to the predetermined result. If the result is uncertain, the process feels pointless. That's an enormous amount of present-moment experience being discarded in service of a future that may or may not arrive in the form you expected.

The practical transformation here is learning to invest in process rather than outcome, and in values rather than results. This doesn't happen through a single insight. It happens through a specific practice of redirecting your attention, repeatedly and deliberately, from the destination to the direction.

Here's how to do this concretely. Take one goal you're currently working toward, ideally one where you notice a lot of anxiety or rigidity around the outcome. Write it down. Now, underneath it, write the values that are driving that goal. Not the result you want, but the qualities and commitments that make this goal meaningful to you. If the goal is to launch a business, the values underneath it might be creativity, financial independence, contribution, or self-determination. If the goal is to improve your health, the values might be vitality, discipline, or being present for the people you love. If the goal is to advance in your career, the values might be mastery, impact, or recognition.

Now ask yourself this question: if the outcome doesn't arrive in the exact form I've imagined, can I still express these values through the process of working toward it? In almost every case, the answer is yes. The values are accessible right now, in today's work, regardless of whether the final result matches your expectations. And when you transformation your primary investment from the outcome to the values, something changes. The work itself becomes meaningful rather than just instrumental. The setbacks become information rather than verdicts. The unexpected turns become part of the story rather than evidence that the story is ruined.

This is what it means to strive with passion while remaining unhooked from the need for a specific predetermined result. You're not less committed. You're committed to something more durable than a single outcome. You're committed to who you're being in the process, to the values you're expressing through your effort, to the kind of work and engagement you're bringing to each day. That commitment doesn't collapse when a plan changes. It doesn't shatter when a result doesn't materialize. It adapts, because it's anchored to something that doesn't depend on external circumstances to remain valid.

There's a second practice worth building here,

specifically for the moments when attachment to an outcome is creating real-time anxiety or paralysis. Call it the "graceful letting go" practice. When you notice yourself gripping a specific result, do this three-step sequence.

First, name the attachment out loud or in writing: "I'm attached to the outcome of [specific result]." Be precise. Not "I want this to go well" but "I'm attached to getting this specific response, this specific number, this specific reaction."

Second, identify what you're afraid will happen if the outcome doesn't arrive: "If this doesn't happen, I'm afraid it means [specific fear]." Get it all the way out. Don't stop at the surface.

Third, redirect to the value: "The value underneath this goal is [specific value], and I can express that value regardless of how this particular outcome turns out."

Do this sequence slowly. It takes about five minutes when you do it properly. What it accomplishes is a real-time loosening of the grip. You're not pretending the outcome doesn't matter. You're relocating your sense of meaning from the outcome to something that's actually within your control: the quality and direction of your engagement. That relocation is the practical experience of attachment reduction.

Over time, this practice changes your baseline relationship to uncertainty. You stop needing conditions to be perfect before you can function. You stop needing the outcome to be guaranteed before you can commit. You stop waiting for external confirmation that your efforts are worthwhile. The internal structure that was previously dependent on specific results becomes anchored instead to values that are available in every moment, regardless of what's happening outside you. That's what operating above your emotions actually requires at this level. Not the absence of preferences, but the freedom to act without being held hostage by them.

Putting It Into Practice

This chapter has covered three interconnected transformations: loosening your grip on rigid self-narratives, de-centering the labels that constrain your behavior, and releasing your investment in predetermined outcomes. Each one addresses a different layer of attachment. Together, they move you toward a kind of psychological freedom that neither defusion nor experiential expansion alone can produce. You need all three layers working together.

The action steps below are built to be done in sequence over the next ten days. They're specific, and each one has a clear, observable outcome so you know when you've actually done it rather than just thought about doing it.

Action step one: Write your three non-negotiable internal rules. Do this today, before the day's demands take over. Sit with a pen and paper for ten minutes. Write down the three internal rules that, when violated, produce the strongest suffering in you. Use the format: "Things should be [X]" or "I need to be [Y] in order to be okay." Be honest. These are the attachments that are currently costing you the most. Once you have them written, put them somewhere you'll see them over the next ten days. You're not trying to eliminate them immediately. You're making them visible so they stop operating invisibly.

Action step two: Run the three-day label de-

centering process. Choose one label from your current self-concept that you suspect has been limiting your behavior. Follow the three-day sequence described earlier in this chapter exactly: day one, build the case for the label; day two, find the contradictions; day three, write and read aloud the both/and statement. Don't skip day two because it feels uncomfortable. That's the most important day. The contradictions your mind resists finding are the ones that carry the most power to loosen the label's grip.

Action step three: Map one goal to its underlying values. Pick the goal that's currently generating the most anxiety or rigidity for you. Write it down. Underneath it, identify the three to five values that make this goal meaningful. Then write one specific thing you can do today that expresses those values, regardless of whether it moves the outcome forward in any measurable way. Do that thing. This single action begins the practical transformation from outcome-investment to value-investment. It gives you a direct experience of what it feels like to do meaningful work without needing the result to validate the effort.

Action step four: Practice the graceful letting

go sequence once a day for seven days. Each day, identify one attachment that's active for you right now, something you're gripping tightly. Run the three-step sequence: name the attachment precisely, identify the underlying fear, redirect to the value. Write it out rather than just thinking it. The writing matters because it forces specificity, and specificity is what separates a genuine practice from a vague intention. By day seven, you'll have worked through seven distinct attachments. You'll have direct evidence that your sense of meaning doesn't collapse when you loosen your grip on a specific result. That evidence is what makes the transformation durable rather than temporary.

The work in this chapter connects directly to everything you've built in the previous two. Defusion created distance from your thoughts. Experiential expansion built your capacity to hold difficult feelings. Attachment reduction removes the conditions you've been unconsciously requiring before you allow yourself to function fully. When those conditions are gone, when you no longer need to feel ready, be labeled correctly, or have the outcome secured before you move, you discover something that's been there all along. The capacity to act from your values right now, in this moment, exactly as things are. That capacity is what the next chapter's work is built on.

Chapter Six

Intentional Action: Your Internal Compass

You've done serious work to get here. You've

learned to step back from your thoughts instead of being swallowed by them. You've built the capacity to feel difficult emotions without running from them. You've loosened the grip on the rigid conditions you used to require before allowing yourself to move. All of that work has been clearing the ground. This chapter is about what you build on it.

Intentional action is where everything becomes real.

Defusion, experiential expansion, and attachment reduction are internal processes. They change your relationship to your own mind. But at some point, you have to do something with that changed relationship. You have to take what you've built on the inside and express it in the actual choices you make, the work you show up for, the conversations you have, the commitments you keep. *That's what intentional action means.* It's the point where transcendent functioning stops being a concept you understand and becomes a life you're actually living.

The reason so many people who understand these ideas still don't change is that they treat the internal work as the destination. They get better at observing their thoughts. They get more comfortable with discomfort. They loosen their attachments. And then they wait. They wait to feel aligned. They wait to feel ready. They wait for some internal signal that it's time to move. That signal rarely comes the way they're expecting it. The gap between insight and action doesn't close on its own. You have to close it deliberately, with specific behaviors that are tied to something more durable than your current emotional state.

That's what this chapter gives you. A clear way to identify what actually matters to you, a method for acting on that even when conditions are difficult, and a practice for getting back on course when you drift. Not as inspiration, but as a working system.

Clarifying Your North Star

Most people, when asked what they want, describe outcomes. A promotion. A better relationship. More confidence. Less anxiety. These are goals, and goals are useful. But goals have a problem that most people don't notice until they're deep inside the pursuit of one. Goals are destinations. They exist in the future. You haven't reached them yet, which means, by definition, you're always somewhere other than where you want to be. When your sense of meaning depends on reaching the goal, you're always one step behind your own life.

Values are different. A value isn't a destination. It's a direction. It's not something you achieve and then possess. It's something you express through the way you engage with what's in front of you right now. Honesty isn't a goal you reach. It's something you can live out in this conversation, today. Creativity isn't a milestone you hit. It's something you bring to the work you're doing this morning. Connection isn't a state you arrive at. It's something you choose in each interaction. *Values are always accessible*, regardless of where you are in relation to your goals. That's what makes them a compass rather than a destination.

This distinction matters more than it might seem at first. When you're operating from goals alone, you're constantly measuring the gap between where you are and where you want to be. That gap produces anxiety, impatience, and a low-grade sense of inadequacy that follows you everywhere. When you're operating from values, the question transformations entirely. You're no longer asking "am I there yet?" You're asking "am I being who I want to be right now?" And that question is always answerable, regardless of external circumstances.

Think about someone like Tomás, a hypothetical 38-year-old entrepreneur who has been building a company for four years. He has clear goals, revenue targets, team milestones, product launches. He works hard and he's made real progress. But he's noticed something unsettling. Even when he hits a goal, the satisfaction lasts about a week before the next target takes over. *He's perpetually behind his own expectations.* He snaps at his team when things slow down. He's stopped enjoying the work itself because the work has become purely instrumental, a means to the next outcome.

What Tomás hasn't done is identify what he actually values underneath all those goals. When he finally does that work, he realizes that what drives him isn't the revenue number. It's the value of building something that genuinely helps people. That value was accessible on day one of his company, and it's accessible on a slow Tuesday when nothing is going right.

When Tomás starts making decisions from that value rather than from the anxiety of the gap between his current reality and his targets, something transformations/changes. He's still ambitious. He still wants the company to succeed. But he's no longer held hostage by the distance between now and the goal.

Identifying your actual values requires more than a quick brainstorm. Most people, when asked to list their values, write down words that sound right. Integrity. Growth. Family. Health. These aren't wrong, but they're often surface-level. They're the values you think you should have rather than the ones that actually drive your behavior.

Real values show up in what you do when it's hard, in what you feel genuinely angry about when it's violated, in what you'd keep doing even if nobody was watching or rewarding you for it.

To get to your real values, you need to go deeper than a list. Work through these questions in writing, one at a time, giving each one at least five minutes of honest reflection. Don't rush them. The answers that come quickly are often the socially acceptable ones. The answers that matter usually take a little longer to surface.

First: Think about a moment in your life when you felt most alive and most yourself. Not necessarily happy, but genuinely you. What were you doing? What made that moment feel real? What does that tell you about what you care about at a deep level?

Second: Think about a time when you felt genuinely angry or deeply troubled by something. Not irritated, but truly bothered. What was being violated in that situation? What does that reaction tell you about what you consider non-negotiable?

Third: If you stripped away every external expectation, every opinion of people whose approval you want, every "should" that's been handed to you by your family, your culture, or your industry, what would you still choose to spend your time on? What would you still care about?

Fourth: When you imagine yourself at the end of your life, looking back with genuine satisfaction, what are the qualities you want to have expressed consistently? Not the achievements you want to have collected, but the kind of person you want to have been.

Write your answers to these questions. Then read through what you've written and look for patterns. The words and themes that keep appearing across multiple answers are pointing at something real. Those are your actual values, not the curated version, but the ones that live underneath your behavior whether you've named them or not.

Once you have two or three clear values identified, write each one as a single short phrase that describes how you want to engage with life. Not "I value honesty" but "I speak truthfully even when it's uncomfortable." Not "I value growth" but "I engage seriously with things that challenge me." The action-oriented phrasing matters because it points directly toward behavior. A value stated as a noun is something you believe in. A value stated as a behavior is something you can do today.

These values are your north star. Not because they give you a fixed destination, but because they give you a consistent direction. On the days when your goals feel far away, when motivation is low, when the external feedback isn't coming, your values are still there. They don't require good conditions to be relevant. They're available right now, in whatever situation you're currently in, waiting to guide your next choice.

Executing in the Presence of Resistance

Knowing your values is necessary. Acting on them is a separate skill entirely.

The gap between knowing and doing is where most people get stuck. You know what matters to you and you know what you should be working on. You know the conversation you need to have, the work you need to start, the habit you need to build. And yet, when the moment arrives, something stops you. You feel tired. You feel anxious. You feel unmotivated. You feel like the conditions aren't right. You tell yourself you'll do it when you're in a better headspace, when things settle down, when you have more energy. And the waiting becomes its own kind of life.

Transcendent functioning doesn't require the absence of resistance. It requires the ability to act in its presence.

This is the central insight of committed action, a concept rooted in Acceptance and Commitment Therapy and central to the TFM model. Committed action means taking steps toward what you value not because you feel ready or motivated or calm, but because the action is aligned with what matters to you.

The action isn't contingent on the feeling. The feeling is allowed to be present while the action happens anyway. This isn't about forcing yourself through gritted teeth and white-knuckling it. It's about recognizing that waiting for the right internal conditions is itself a choice, and it's a choice that keeps you in place.

Think about what this actually looks like in practice. You value honest communication, but you've been avoiding a difficult conversation with someone at work because the anxiety around it feels too high. Committed action doesn't wait for the anxiety to drop before initiating the conversation. It acknowledges the anxiety, notes that the conversation is aligned with the value of honesty, and initiates anyway. The anxiety is present. The action happens regardless. That's not recklessness. That's the practical application of everything you've built in the previous chapters.

Defusion created distance from the thought that the conversation will go badly. Experiential expansion built your capacity to hold the anxiety without fleeing it. Attachment reduction loosened your grip on needing the conversation to go a specific way. Committed action is what you do with all of that space.

The most common obstacle to committed action isn't laziness or lack of discipline. It's the belief, usually unconscious, that you need to feel a certain way before the action is appropriate. This belief is so widespread that most people don't even recognize it as a belief. It just feels like common sense. Of course you should wait until you feel ready. Of course you should act when you're motivated. But when you examine it honestly, you'll notice that "feeling ready" is not a reliable signal. It doesn't arrive on schedule. It doesn't appear before important things. It tends to show up, if at all, after you've already started moving. The readiness follows the action. It doesn't precede it.

To make committed action practical and sustainable, you need a planning structure that bridges the gap between your values and your daily behavior (Hayes et al., 2006). SMART goals are a widely used structure, and they work well here when they're built from values rather than from external pressure or comparison (Doran, 1981). A SMART goal is Specific, Measurable, Achievable, Relevant, and Time-bound.

Most people know this framework. The piece that's often missing is the values connection. A goal built purely on external metrics can be abandoned when motivation drops, because there's nothing underneath it that's durable. A goal built from a genuine value has a different quality. When resistance shows up, you have something to anchor to beyond the feeling of wanting to succeed (Hayes et al., 2006).

Here's how to build a value-driven SMART plan for one area of your life where you've been inconsistent.

Start by choosing one of the values you identified in the previous section. Write it at the top of a page. Underneath it, write one specific behavior that would express that value over the next two weeks. Make it concrete enough that you could tell someone else exactly what you did and they'd understand it clearly. "Work on my project" is not specific enough. "Write for thirty minutes each morning before opening email" is specific. "Be more present with my family" is not specific enough. "Put my phone in a drawer from 6pm to 8pm on weekdays and spend that time engaged with my family" is specific.

Now check it against the SMART criteria. Is it specific enough to know when you've done it? Is it measurable so you can track it? Is it achievable given your current life, not the ideal version of your life, but the actual one? Is it relevant to the value you identified? And is there a clear time boundary, two weeks, thirty days, one week, so it doesn't just float indefinitely? If it passes all five, write it as a commitment: "For the next fourteen days, I will [specific behavior] because I value [specific value]." The "because" matters. It ties the behavior to something durable. When resistance shows up on day seven, the "because" is what you come back to.

There's a specific technique for the moments when resistance is highest, when you're standing at the edge of the action and everything in you wants to step back. It's called the two-minute rule, and it works by removing the requirement that you commit to the full action before you start. You only commit to two minutes. Two minutes of writing. Two minutes of the difficult conversation. Two minutes of the workout. Two minutes of the focused work. Two minutes is almost always achievable regardless of how you feel and what happens in those two minutes, almost without exception, is that momentum builds. The resistance was at the threshold. Once you're past it, the action becomes easier. Not easy. Easier. The two-minute rule doesn't make the work feel good. It makes starting it accessible regardless of how you feel.

One more thing worth saying clearly about executing in the presence of resistance. *You don't need to feel aligned with your values to act on them.* Alignment is a feeling, and feelings fluctuate. There will be days when acting on your values feels meaningful and energizing. There will be more days when it feels like effort, like going through motions, like doing the right thing without any emotional reward for it. Both kinds of days count equally. The action on the difficult day is not less valuable than the action on the inspired day. In fact, it might be more valuable, because it's building the specific capacity that transcendent functioning requires: the ability to act from your values when your emotions aren't cooperating. That capacity doesn't get built on the easy days. It gets built on the hard ones.

Maintaining Integrity and Self-Correction

You will drift. This isn't pessimism. It's an honest description of what happens when human beings try to sustain any kind of meaningful change over time. You'll have a strong week where your actions line up closely with your values. Then something will happen. A stressful period at work. A personal difficulty. A stretch of poor sleep. A run of setbacks that makes the whole effort feel pointless. And you'll find yourself back in old patterns, reactive, avoidant, inconsistent. Acting in ways that don't reflect who you're trying to be.

What you do in that moment determines almost everything.

Most people respond to a drift in one of two ways. The first is self-punishment. They turn the drift into evidence of a deeper failure. "I knew I couldn't sustain this." "I always do this." "I'm just not the kind of person who follows through." The self-criticism feels like accountability, but it isn't. It's just suffering layered on top of the original drift, and it makes returning to the path significantly harder. You can't shame yourself into better behavior. You can exhaust yourself with shame while the behavior stays the same.

The second response is denial. They minimize the drift, tell themselves it wasn't that significant, avoid looking at it clearly. This feels better in the short term, but it means you don't learn anything from what happened. The same drift happens again, for the same reasons, and you're no more equipped to handle it than you were the first time.

There's a third response, and it's the one that actually works. It's called self-compassion with accountability, and it requires doing two things simultaneously that most people think are contradictory. You acknowledge the drift honestly, without minimizing it, and you treat yourself with the same basic decency you'd offer someone you care about who was struggling. Not because you deserve a pass, but because harsh self-judgment doesn't produce better behavior. It produces avoidance, shame spirals, and the kind of all-or-nothing thinking that makes people abandon good work over a single imperfect week.

Research by Kristin Neff at the University of Texas has consistently shown that self-compassion is associated with greater motivation to improve, not less. People who treat themselves with compassion after a setback are more likely to try again, not less. The intuition that you need to be hard on yourself to stay accountable is simply wrong.

What you need is honest acknowledgment paired with the belief that returning to your values is possible and worth doing. Self-compassion provides the second part. Without it, the honest acknowledgment just becomes another reason to give up.

Here's a specific self-correction practice to use whenever you notice you've drifted. It takes about ten minutes and works best done in writing. Start by naming what happened without drama or minimizing. Not "I've completely failed at everything I was trying to do" and not "it wasn't really that bad." Just: "For the past [specific period], I've been [specific behavior that's out of alignment with my values]." Be precise. "I've been avoiding the project I said I'd work on daily" is useful. "I've been slipping" is not.

Second, identify what got in the way. Not as an excuse, but as information. Was it a specific trigger? A particular kind of stress? A situation that made your old patterns feel necessary? Understanding the mechanism of the drift is what allows you to respond to it differently next time. If you don't know why you drifted, you'll drift in the same way again under the same conditions.

Third, write one sentence that acknowledges the drift with self-compassion. "I got pulled off course, and that makes sense given what I was dealing with, and I'm choosing to come back." Say it out loud. It might feel awkward. Say it anyway. The act of speaking that sentence interrupts the shame spiral and redirects your attention toward the next move rather than the failed one.

Fourth, identify one specific action you can take today that expresses the value you drifted from. Not a grand re-commitment. Not a new system. Just one action, today, that puts you back in contact with what matters. The return doesn't need to be dramatic. It just needs to be real.

This practice treats your life as what it actually is: an iterative process. Not a performance you either pass or fail, but an ongoing series of choices, some of which will be well-aligned with your values and some of which won't. The goal isn't a perfect record. The goal is a pattern that trends toward alignment over time, with the ability to notice when you've drifted and return without making the drift into a catastrophe.

There's another layer to maintaining integrity that goes beyond handling setbacks. It's about the ongoing practice of noticing when your behavior is drifting out of alignment before it becomes a significant drift. This is what "living awake" actually means in practice. Not a dramatic state of constant enlightenment, but the simple, daily habit of checking in with yourself honestly. Are my actions today reflecting what I said matters to me? Not perfectly, but directionally. Are the choices I'm making this week moving me toward the life I want to be building, or away from it?

A brief daily integrity check is one of the most powerful practices in this entire book, and it takes less than three minutes. At the end of each day, ask yourself three questions. First: what did I do today that was aligned with my values? Name something specific. Even on a difficult day, there's usually something. Second: what did I do today that wasn't aligned? Be honest. Don't skip this one because it's uncomfortable. Third: what's one thing I'll do differently tomorrow? Not a list of improvements. One thing. Specific and achievable.

Write the answers down. The writing matters because it creates a record. Over time, that record becomes a genuine map of how you're actually living versus how you intend to live. Patterns become visible. You start to see which situations consistently pull you off course. You start to see which values you're expressing consistently and which ones you keep saying matter but rarely act on. That information is more valuable than any amount of motivational content, because it's specific to you, based on your actual behavior, and it points directly to where your work needs to go next.

The deeper principle underneath all of this is that integrity isn't a trait you either have or don't have. It's a practice. It's the ongoing, imperfect, daily effort to close the gap between who you say you are and how you actually behave. That gap will never be zero. But it can be small, and it can keep getting smaller, if you're willing to look at it honestly and return to your values without making the looking into a punishment.

Every choice you make is a chance to live with intention. Not every choice will be the right one. But every choice is an opportunity to be awake to what you're doing and why. That wakefulness, practiced consistently, is what separates a life that happens to you from a life you're actually building.

Your Next Move

Everything in this chapter points toward one thing: the active, daily practice of living from your values rather than from the weather of your internal state. Intentional action is the place where transcendent functioning becomes visible in the world. It's where the internal transformations you've made in the previous chapters translate into actual choices, actual work, actual relationships, actual results.

The following steps are designed to be done in a specific sequence. Each one builds directly on the last. Don't treat them as a menu to pick from. Work through them in order.

Step one: Identify your top three values using the four questions from the first section of this chapter. Do this today, in writing, giving each question at least five minutes of honest reflection. When you're done, write each value as a single action-oriented phrase. Not a noun. A behavior. "I speak honestly even when it's uncomfortable." "I engage seriously with work that challenges me." "I show up for the people I care about even when I'm tired." These three phrases are your compass. Put them somewhere you'll see them every morning.

Step two: For each of your three values, identify one micro-action you can take today. Not a project. Not a plan. One small, specific behavior that expresses that value before the day is over. If your value is honest communication, the micro-action might be sending a message you've been putting off because it feels awkward. If your value is creative engagement, the micro-action might be spending twenty minutes on something you care about before opening your inbox. If your value is physical vitality, the micro-action might be a ten-minute walk you take regardless of how you feel. Do all three today. Not because they'll change your life in a day, but because doing them gives you direct, lived experience of what it feels like to act from your values rather than wait for the right conditions.

Step three: Build one value-driven SMART commitment for the next two weeks. Choose the value that feels most urgent or most neglected right now. Using the structure from the second section of this chapter, write a specific, measurable, achievable, relevant, time-bound commitment that expresses that value over the next fourteen days. Write it in the format: "For the next fourteen days, I will [specific behavior] because I value [specific value]." Post it somewhere visible. Tell one person about it if you can. External accountability, even minimal, significantly increases follow-through on new commitments.

Step four: Set up your daily integrity check. Choose a consistent time each evening, even five minutes before you go to sleep, and ask yourself the three questions from the third section: what did I do today that was aligned with my values, what wasn't, and what's one thing I'll do differently tomorrow. Write the answers in a notebook. Keep the notebook next to your bed so the habit has a physical anchor. Do this every day for the next thirty days without exception. At the end of thirty days, read back through what you've written. The patterns you'll see will tell you more about how you're actually living than any amount of self-reflection done without a record.

Step five: Practice the self-correction sequence the next time you drift. You don't need to wait for a major setback. The next time you notice yourself acting out of alignment with one of your values, even in a small way, run the four-step sequence from the third section. Name what happened specifically. Identify what got in the way. Write one sentence of honest, compassionate acknowledgment. Take one action today that expresses the value you drifted from. Do this within twenty-four hours of noticing the drift. The speed of the return matters more than the perfection of the return.

These five steps aren't complicated. What makes them powerful is consistency. The person who does them imperfectly but regularly will build something real. The person who understands them but waits for the right moment to start will stay exactly where they are. The right moment is now, with the values you've identified, in the life you're actually living, with the resistance that's actually present. That's always been the only moment available. And it's enough.

Chapter Seven

Level 1: Understanding Reactive Functioning

Before you can operate above your emotions, you need to understand what it looks like when your emotions are operating you. That's what this chapter is about.

Not in a theoretical way, but in the specific, recognizable, sometimes uncomfortable way that shows up in your actual daily life. The patterns described here aren't character flaws. They're the default setting. They're what happens when nobody teaches you anything different, and when the part of your brain designed to keep you safe gets handed the controls for your entire life.

Most people are living reactively without knowing it. They experience it as just being themselves and that's the first thing worth understanding. Reactive functioning doesn't feel like a problem from the inside. It feels like reality. When you avoid a difficult conversation because it makes you anxious, it doesn't feel like avoidance. It feels like a reasonable decision. When you procrastinate on important work because starting it feels uncomfortable, it doesn't feel like a reactive pattern. It feels like waiting until you're ready. When you snap at someone because you're stressed, it doesn't feel like your nervous system hijacking your behavior. It feels like a justified response. The reactive mode is invisible to the person inside it, which is exactly what makes it so persistent.

This chapter is going to make it visible.

The Reflexive Life

Your brain has a threat detection system that's been running for hundreds of thousands of years. It's called the *amygdala*, and its entire job is to scan your environment for anything that might hurt you and trigger a response before your conscious mind has time to weigh in. In the ancestral environment, this system was essential. A rustle in the grass could mean a predator. A distant stick on the ground could be a snake. The half-second advantage of an automatic fear response was the difference between survival and death. The system didn't need to be accurate. It needed to be fast.

The problem is that you're not living in that environment anymore.

Your threat detector didn't get the memo. It still fires with the same urgency it used for predators, but now it fires for emails from your boss, for the moment before a presentation, for a text message that takes too long to get a response, for any situation that carries even a hint of social rejection, failure, or loss of control. The signal is the same. The full-body alarm, the racing heart, the narrowed focus, the urge to act immediately. But the threats are different, and the responses that served your ancestors don't serve you nearly as well in a modern life.

This is the core of reactive functioning. Your automatic systems respond to internal cues, feelings of threat, discomfort, uncertainty, or overwhelm, with behaviors designed to make those feelings stop as quickly as possible. Avoid the thing that triggers anxiety. Escape the situation that produces shame. Shut down when the overwhelm becomes too much. Attack when you feel backed into a corner. These responses happen fast, often before you've consciously decided anything. By the time you're aware of what you're doing, you're already doing it.

Think about what a typical reactive day actually looks like:

You wake up and check your phone before you've been conscious for sixty seconds, because the low-grade anxiety of not knowing what's waiting for you is uncomfortable.

You open an email that requires a difficult response and close it immediately, telling yourself you'll deal with it later.

You sit down to work on something important and find yourself doing three easier tasks first, because the important one produces a feeling of inadequacy that you'd rather not feel.

You have a conversation where someone says something that triggers a flash of defensiveness, and you respond from that defensiveness rather than from any considered position.

By the end of the day, you've made dozens of decisions, and a significant portion of them were made not by you, but by whatever feeling was loudest in that moment.

That's the reflexive life. A life where the internal

cues are pulling the strings, and the person attached to those strings is mostly just along for the ride.

Consider a hypothetical scenario: someone like Ryan, a 29-year-old freelance writer who's been struggling with inconsistency for most of his adult life. He's talented, and he knows it. He gets excited about projects, commits to them with genuine enthusiasm, and then finds himself stalling out somewhere in the middle. He checks social media when he should be writing. He takes on new projects to escape the discomfort of finishing existing ones. He avoids pitching his work to bigger publications because the possibility of rejection produces a feeling he'd rather not deal with.

Ryan doesn't experience any of this as avoidance. He experiences it as a creative process, as waiting for inspiration, as being selective about opportunities. He has a sophisticated explanation for every reactive pattern he runs.

The explanations feel true from the inside. But the result, year after year, is a gap between what he's capable of and what he's actually producing. The puppet strings are invisible to him, but they're real, and they're running his professional life.

Ryan's situation isn't unusual. It's the norm. The specific content differs from person to person, but the structure is the same. Internal discomfort triggers automatic behavior. The behavior reduces the discomfort temporarily. The pattern gets reinforced. The world gets a little smaller. Repeat.

The "shrinking world" effect is one of the most important consequences of chronic reactive functioning, and it happens so gradually that most people don't notice it until the shrinkage is significant.

Each avoidance feels like a single, isolated, reasonable choice. But avoidance is cumulative. Every time you skip the difficult conversation, the difficult conversation becomes harder to have. Every time you avoid the high-stakes opportunity, the high-stakes opportunity becomes more threatening.

Every time you retreat from discomfort, your definition of what's tolerable narrows slightly. Over months and years, the range of situations you can engage with comfortably gets smaller and smaller, while the range of situations that trigger your threat detector gets larger and larger. You end up living in an increasingly defended, increasingly limited version of your own life, and the defense feels so normal that you've stopped questioning it.

Recognizing the puppet strings of your own reactive habits requires a specific kind of attention. Not judgment, but honest observation. The question to ask yourself isn't "am I a reactive person?" That framing leads nowhere useful. The question is: "in which specific situations do I consistently act from my feelings rather than from a considered choice?"

Those situations are where your reactive patterns live. They're the places where the amygdala has learned to take over, and where your conscious values have learned to step aside.

Start noticing those situations this week. Not to fix them yet. Just to see them. The moment you can see a reactive pattern clearly, you've already created a small amount of space between you and it. That space is where everything else in this book becomes possible.

Mechanisms of Reactivity: Fusion and Avoidance

Knowing that you're reactive is one thing. Understanding why the pattern is so persistent, why it keeps running even when you can see it and even when you want to change it, is something else. There are two specific mechanisms that keep reactive loops in place. Both of them operate below the level of conscious intention. Both of them feel like protection. And both of them are quietly costing you more than you realize.

The first mechanism is cognitive fusion, which you worked with in depth in Chapter 2. But it's worth revisiting here in the context of reactive functioning specifically, because fusion is the cognitive engine that makes reactivity automatic. When you're fused with a thought, you don't experience it as a thought. You experience it as reality. "This is going to go badly" isn't a prediction your mind is generating. It's a fact about the future. "I can't handle this" isn't a feeling of overwhelm. It's an accurate assessment of your capabilities. "People will judge me for this" isn't an anxious story. It's a reliable forecast.

When thoughts carry that kind of weight, they don't invite reflection. They demand response. And the response is almost always reactive, because the thought has been framed as a genuine threat. You don't deliberate about how to respond to a genuine threat. You react. The fusion turns a mental event into an emergency, and emergencies bypass the parts of your brain responsible for considered, values-based decision-making.

That's not a weakness. It's how the system was designed. The problem is that the system can't distinguish between a genuine emergency and a thought that feels like one.

The second mechanism is avoidance, and it's the behavioral side of the same coin. Avoidance is what you do when a feeling becomes uncomfortable enough that your primary goal transformations from "what do I want to do here?" to "how do I make this feeling stop?"

It's a completely understandable response. Discomfort is unpleasant. Reducing it feels good. And avoidance is remarkably effective at reducing discomfort in the short term. That's exactly what makes it so destructive over time.

Here's the mechanism in plain terms. You encounter a situation that produces discomfort. You avoid it. The discomfort drops. Your brain registers this sequence: discomfort appeared, avoidance made it go away, avoidance was the right move. The next time a similar situation appears, the avoidance response fires faster and with more force, because it's been reinforced. The discomfort itself becomes more alarming, because your brain has been consistently treating it as something that requires immediate escape. The avoidance behavior becomes more automatic, and the situations that trigger it expand, because your nervous system has learned to generalize. What started as avoiding one specific uncomfortable thing gradually becomes a broader pattern of avoiding anything that produces a similar feeling.

This is the cycle that keeps people stuck at the reactive level of functioning, and it operates through a principle called negative reinforcement. Negative reinforcement doesn't mean punishment. It means that a behavior gets strengthened because it removes something unpleasant. Every time avoidance successfully removes discomfort, the avoidance behavior gets stronger. The temporary relief is the reinforcement. And because the relief is immediate while the costs are gradual and cumulative, the reinforcement wins every time. Your brain is optimizing for short-term comfort in a situation that requires long-term engagement. The math is completely wrong for the life you're trying to build.

There's a subtler layer to avoidance that's worth understanding clearly. Avoidance isn't always obvious. It doesn't always look like canceling plans or refusing to try something. It can look like staying extremely busy so you never have to sit with a difficult feeling. It can look like researching endlessly instead of starting. It can look like having the same conversation with a friend about a problem you never actually address. It can look like perfectionism, where the standard is set so high that you never have to risk genuine exposure. These are all avoidance.

They all serve the same function: keeping you away from a feeling that your nervous system has flagged as dangerous. And they all carry the same long-term cost: a life organized around what you're avoiding rather than what you're moving toward.

Low metacognitive awareness is what allows both of these mechanisms to keep running unchecked. Metacognition is your ability to think about your own thinking, to observe your mental processes rather than just being inside them. Most people have relatively low metacognitive awareness in their day-to-day lives, not because they're not intelligent, but because nobody taught them to develop it. They're aware of what they're thinking and feeling. They're much less aware of the patterns those thoughts and feelings are creating in their behavior over time.

Without metacognitive awareness, you can't see the difference between a genuine choice and an automatic reaction. Both feel like decisions. The person who avoids a difficult conversation genuinely believes they're making a reasonable call about timing.

The person who procrastinates on important work genuinely believes they're managing their energy. The person who stays in a situation that isn't serving them genuinely believes they're being realistic. The reactive pattern has a story, and from inside the pattern, the story feels completely coherent. Metacognitive awareness is what lets you step back far enough to see the pattern rather than just the story.

Reactivity is, at its core, a lack of conscious

choice. That's the key insight to carry forward. When you're reactive, you're not choosing your response. You're running a program. The stimulus arrives, the program executes, the behavior happens. The program was written by your history, your conditioning, your nervous system's threat assessments, your early experiences with what's safe and what isn't. It wasn't written by your values. It wasn't written by the person you're trying to become. And until you can see it clearly enough to step outside of it, even briefly, it will keep running regardless of how much you know about psychology or how motivated you are to change.

This is why insight alone doesn't produce change. You can understand reactive functioning completely and still be reactive, because understanding it and interrupting it in real time are completely different skills. The understanding is necessary but not sufficient. What you need alongside the understanding is the ability to create a pause between the stimulus and the response. A moment, however brief, where you can observe what's happening and choose your next move rather than simply executing the automatic one. That pause is what the rest of this book is built on. But you can only create it if you can first see clearly when and where the automatic responses are running.

Fusion keeps you locked in by making thoughts feel like facts. Avoidance keeps you locked in by making relief feel like progress. Together, they create a closed loop that's remarkably self-sustaining. The thought triggers discomfort. The discomfort triggers avoidance. The avoidance provides temporary relief. The relief reinforces the avoidance. The next similar thought triggers even faster discomfort, because the pattern has been practiced. The loop tightens. And the person inside it experiences all of this as just the way things are, as their personality, as their limitations, as reality itself.

It's none of those things. It's a learned pattern. And learned patterns can be interrupted.

The interruption begins with awareness, which is why the next section focuses specifically on building that awareness in a structured, practical way. You can't work with what you can't see. The trigger log you'll build in the action steps below is the tool for making the invisible visible. Once you can see your reactive patterns clearly, named and specific and documented, you have something you can actually work with. The pattern is no longer just something that happens to you. It's something you can observe, examine, and eventually choose differently.

That choice, made deliberately in a moment that previously would have been automatic, is the first real step toward transcendent functioning. Not the dramatic transformation, not the permanent transformation, but the small, specific, real moment where you catch yourself mid-reaction and recognize it for what it is. That moment is the crack in the wall. Everything else gets built from there.

Putting It Into Practice

Understanding *reactive functioning* intellectually is the starting point. The real work is building enough self-awareness to catch your own patterns in real time. The practices below are designed to do exactly that over the next forty-eight hours and beyond. They're not complicated. They require honesty and consistency more than anything else.

Practice one: Keep a trigger log for 48 hours

starting today. This is the most important thing you can do right now, and it's more specific than it sounds. Get a small notebook or open a notes app you'll actually use. Every time you notice yourself acting on impulse, every time you avoid something uncomfortable, every time you react to a feeling rather than making a considered choice, write down four things. First, what was the situation? Be specific. Not "I was stressed at work" but "I was sitting at my desk with the report open and I switched to checking email instead." Second, what was the feeling or internal cue that triggered the reaction? Anxiety, boredom, irritation, a flash of self-doubt, a sense of dread. Name it as precisely as you can. Third, what did you do? The specific behavior. Not "I avoided it" but "I closed the tab and made coffee instead." Fourth, what was the result? Did the feeling drop temporarily? Did you feel relieved, then guilty, then back to where you started?

Do this for every reactive moment you notice over forty-eight hours. You won't catch all of them. You'll catch some, and that's enough. The goal isn't a complete record. The goal is to start seeing the pattern. By the end of forty-eight hours, you'll have a concrete, specific list of the situations, feelings, and behaviors that make up your personal reactive loop. That list is more valuable than any amount of general self-knowledge, because it's specific to you, based on your actual behavior, and it points directly to where your work needs to go.

Practice two: After the 48 hours, identify your top three reactive triggers. Read through your log and look for patterns. Which feelings showed up most often? Which situations consistently produced reactive behavior? Which avoidance behaviors did you reach for most automatically? Circle the three entries that feel most significant, either because they happen most frequently or because the cost of the reaction is highest. Write those three patterns on a separate page using this format: "When I feel [specific feeling] in [specific type of situation], I tend to [specific reactive behavior]." For example: "When I feel the first wave of anxiety about a task, I tend to switch to something easier and tell myself I'll come back to it." That sentence, written clearly, is already a form of metacognitive awareness. You've stepped back far enough to describe the pattern from the outside rather than just experiencing it from the inside.

Practice three: For each of your three patterns,

identify the short-term payoff and the long-term cost. This step is critical because it makes the reinforcement cycle visible. For each pattern, write one sentence describing what the avoidance gives you immediately. The relief, the escape from discomfort, the temporary sense of control. Then write one sentence describing what it costs you over time. The narrowed options, the unfinished work, the relationship damage, the gap between who you're being and who you want to be. Seeing both sides of the equation clearly is what begins to transformation the cost-benefit calculation your brain has been running automatically. When the long-term cost is invisible, the short-term relief always wins. When you can see both, you have the beginning of a real choice.

Practice four: Create one "pause point" for your most frequent reactive pattern. From your list of three, pick the pattern that shows up most often in your daily life. Now design a specific, concrete pause for it. A pause point is a pre-decided action you take in the moment between the trigger and the reactive behavior. It needs to be simple enough to actually use under pressure. Some examples: before closing the difficult email, take three slow breaths and read it one more time. Before switching away from the important task, set a two-minute timer and stay with the discomfort for just those two minutes. Before sending the defensive message, write your response in a notes app instead of directly in the message thread, wait ten minutes, then decide whether to send it.

The pause point doesn't have to eliminate the reactive behavior. It just has to insert a moment of awareness between the trigger and the response. That moment is where your conscious choice can enter the equation. Even if you still do the reactive thing after the pause, you've done it consciously rather than automatically. That's a meaningful difference, and it's where the real work begins.

These four practices together do something specific. They move reactive functioning from an invisible, automatic process to something you can observe, name, and begin to work with deliberately. The trigger log gives you data. The pattern identification gives you clarity. The cost-benefit analysis gives you motivation that's grounded in reality rather than willpower. And the pause point gives you a real-time tool for creating the space between stimulus and response that Viktor Frankl described as the location of human freedom.

You won't eliminate reactivity in forty-eight hours. That's not the goal. The goal is to stop being completely inside the pattern and start being able to see it from slightly outside. That transformation in perspective, however small it feels, is the foundation everything else in this book is built on. You can't transcend what you can't see. Now you can see it.

Chapter Eight

Level 2: Mastering Regulated Functioning

You've seen what reactive functioning looks like from the inside. The automatic responses. The feelings running the show. The invisible puppet strings pulling your behavior in directions you didn't consciously choose. If you've been doing the work from the previous chapter, you've started to see your own patterns more clearly. You've named them. You've begun to create small pauses between the trigger and the response. That's real progress, and it matters. But there's a next stage, and most people who do serious self-improvement work end up here without fully realizing what it is or what it costs.

Regulated functioning is where you learn to manage your internal world deliberately. You develop tools. You build strategies. You get genuinely skilled at modulating your emotional state, challenging unhelpful thoughts, and keeping yourself functional even when things feel difficult. This is the level that most therapy, most self-help books, and most productivity systems are designed to get you to. And it's a real step forward from reactive functioning. There's no question about that.

The question this chapter asks is harder. What happens when regulation becomes your entire strategy? What does it cost you to be always managing, always monitoring, always holding things together through deliberate effort? And what does it tell you that the goal of transcendent functioning, operating above your emotions rather than constantly wrestling with them, requires something fundamentally different from even the best regulation skills?

That's what you'll understand by the end of this chapter.

The Effort of Management

Think about what it actually takes to juggle. Not the easy version where you toss two objects back and forth. Real juggling, with three or four items in the air at once. When you first learn, every single catch requires your full conscious attention. You're thinking about each ball individually. Your eyes are darting. Your hands are tense. Your entire focus is consumed by the task of keeping things from hitting the floor. You can do it. But you can't have a conversation while you do it. You can't think about anything else. The juggling takes everything you've got.

Regulated functioning is like that stage of juggling.

You've learned the techniques. Emotional regulation, cognitive restructuring, mindfulness practices, problem-solving strategies. These are real skills and they genuinely work. But at this stage, using them requires effort. Deliberate, conscious, sustained effort. Every time anxiety rises, you apply a technique to bring it down. Every time a negative thought spiral starts, you interrupt it with a reframe. Every time you feel tension building before something important, you run through a calming protocol. The tools work but they require you to be constantly on, constantly monitoring, constantly ready to intervene in your own internal experience before it gets out of hand.

That's a significant cognitive load to carry through every day.

Emotional regulation, as a skill set, involves the ability to influence which emotions you experience, when you experience them, and how intensely you feel them. Research by James Gross at Stanford has identified several core strategies people use: cognitive reappraisal, which means changing how you interpret a situation; attentional deployment, which means deliberately transformationing your focus; and response modulation, which means altering how you express or suppress what you're feeling.

These strategies are well-supported by research. People who use them effectively report lower anxiety, better relationships, and stronger performance across multiple domains. And yet, they all share one common feature. They require you to do something. Actively. In the moment. When your cognitive and emotional resources are already being taxed by whatever situation you're navigating.

Consider a hypothetical scenario: someone like Elena, a 33-year-old team lead at a tech company who has spent two years actively working on her emotional regulation. She's learned to pause before responding in tense meetings. She practices cognitive reappraisal when she gets critical feedback. She uses breathing techniques before high-stakes presentations. By any measure, she's significantly more regulated than she was two years ago. Her team notices it. Her manager has commented on her composure. And yet Elena describes something she can't quite name: a persistent tiredness that doesn't go away no matter how much sleep she gets. A sense that she's always slightly braced, always slightly vigilant, always one difficult situation away from having to deploy her toolkit again. She's functioning well. But she doesn't feel free. She feels like someone who's very good at keeping plates spinning.

Elena's experience is one of the most common and least-discussed aspects of regulated functioning. The tools work. The management is real. But the management itself becomes a kind of weight.

Cognitive restructuring adds another layer to this picture. This is the process of identifying unhelpful thought patterns and actively replacing them with more balanced, realistic ones. If you catch yourself catastrophizing before a difficult conversation, you challenge the thought: what's the actual evidence? What's the realistic outcome? What would I tell a friend who was thinking this way? The technique is grounded in solid cognitive-behavioral research and it produces real results. But it also requires you to maintain a running internal commentary on your own thinking. You become a constant editor of your own mind, watching for distortions, flagging them, correcting them, monitoring whether the correction is holding.

That's exhausting in a way that's hard to describe to someone who hasn't experienced it. It's not dramatic exhaustion. It's the low-grade, cumulative kind. The kind that makes you feel like you've worked hard even on days when nothing particularly challenging happened. Because you have worked hard. You've been managing your internal world all day long.

Problem-solving is the third major tool in the regulated functioning toolkit. When a stressor appears, you don't just react to it and you don't just feel it. You analyze it. You identify what's within your control. You generate options. You choose a course of action. This is genuinely adaptive behavior, and it moves you miles ahead of the reactive mode where the stressor simply triggered an automatic response. But problem-solving also requires mental bandwidth. It requires you to stay in a somewhat analytical relationship with your own experience, treating your internal states as problems to be diagnosed and addressed rather than simply as weather to be observed.

None of these tools are wrong. They're stepping stones, and they're necessary ones. You can't skip regulated functioning on the way to transcendent functioning. The skills you build at this level, the ability to pause before reacting, to challenge distorted thinking, to regulate emotional intensity, these become the foundation for something more fluid and less effortful later on. But you have to understand what this level is and what it isn't. It's a significant upgrade from reactive functioning. It's not the destination.

The destination is a way of operating where you're not spending your day managing yourself. Where the internal weather can be rough without requiring constant intervention. Where you're not monitoring your own emotional state the way a pilot monitors a dashboard, scanning for warning lights, ready to correct at any moment. That kind of functioning exists. It's what this entire book is building toward. And understanding regulated functioning clearly, including its real costs, is what makes the transition to that level possible.

Start paying attention this week to the effort your regulation requires. Not to stop regulating, but to see the cost honestly. Every time you apply a technique to manage your internal state, notice what it takes. Notice the attention it consumes. Notice whether there's a subtle tension underneath the management, a background vigilance that doesn't fully switch off even when things are going well. That noticing isn't a reason to abandon your tools. It's the beginning of understanding why those tools, as valuable as they are, aren't the final answer.

The Paradox of Control

There's something deeply counterintuitive at the heart of regulated functioning, and most people don't see it until they've been managing themselves for long enough to feel the full weight of it. The more skillfully you try to control your internal experience, the more your internal experience becomes the center of your life. The management itself keeps the thing you're managing at the center of your attention.

Think about what it means to be vigilant. Vigilance requires a threat. You can't be vigilant about nothing. When you organize your psychological life around managing your emotional states, you're implicitly treating those states as threats that require constant monitoring. Your anxiety is something to be caught early and brought down before it escalates. Your self-doubt is something to be challenged before it takes hold. Your frustration is something to be processed before it leaks out. The techniques are applied to the threats, and the application keeps the threats salient. Your brain stays focused on the very thing you're trying to manage, because management requires attention, and attention keeps things alive.

This is the paradox. The vigilance that's designed to reduce anxiety can actually amplify it. Research on anxiety disorders indicates that heightened monitoring of internal states, which are commonly described as interoceptive hypervigilance, paradoxically increases sensitivity to those sensations over time, amplifying both their perceived intensity and emotional impact.When you're always watching for anxiety to appear, your threshold for detecting it gets lower. You catch it earlier, which seems like a win, but it also means you're experiencing it more frequently and treating more and more ordinary internal fluctuations as warning signs requiring intervention.

You become, in a very real sense, more anxious about your anxiety.

The "holding it together" quality of regulated functioning creates a second problem that's less about anxiety and more about exhaustion and isolation. When your primary psychological project is maintaining a regulated internal state, that project tends to go underground. You don't talk about it because talking about it would require admitting how much effort it takes. You present as composed because composure is the goal. You handle things because handling things is what you've learned to do. And somewhere in there, the gap between your internal experience and your external presentation gets wider. You're managing on the inside and performing on the outside, and the distance between those two things is its own kind of loneliness.

This isn't a small thing. The research on emotional suppression, which is different from regulation but often gets confused with it, shows consistent associations with reduced social connection, increased physiological stress responses, and greater difficulty in close relationships. When you're spending significant energy managing your internal world, you have less capacity for genuine presence with other people. You're partly elsewhere, partly monitoring, partly braced for the next internal event that requires your attention. *The people around you might not notice. But you feel it.* The conversations that stay on the surface. The moments of connection that don't quite land. The sense that you're showing up, but not fully.

There is also a well-documented paradox in which attempts to exert control over internal experiences can amplify the very states one is trying to manage. Psychologists refer to this as the ironic process effect, where deliberate efforts to suppress thoughts or regulate internal states increase their accessibility and persistence (Wegner, 1994). As discussed in Chapter 2 in the context of thought suppression, this effect is not limited to cognition. Similar patterns have been observed in emotional regulation, where attempts to suppress or tightly control emotional experience can lead to increased physiological arousal and reduced psychological flexibility (Gross & Levenson, 1997; Hayes et al., 2006).

When you set "don't feel anxious" or "don't get

angry" as a goal, the monitoring required to pursue that goal involves repeatedly checking whether the unwanted state is present. The checking itself activates the neural pathways associated with the state you're trying to avoid. You're essentially running a background program that asks "am I anxious yet?" hundreds of times a day, and each time the program runs, it activates a small amount of the very thing it's checking for.

The result, for someone who has been regulating intensively for months or years, can be a strange kind of fatigue. Not the fatigue of someone who hasn't been trying. The fatigue of someone who has been trying very hard, consistently, and is starting to wonder why the trying never seems to produce a lasting sense of ease. They're doing everything right by the standards of regulated functioning. The tools are working. The symptoms are managed. And yet there's a persistent sense of effort, of maintenance, of running to stand still. That sense is accurate. That's exactly what regulated functioning feels like from the inside when you've been doing it for a while.

Understanding this paradox isn't an argument for giving up your regulation skills. It's an argument for understanding their place in the larger picture. Regulation is a necessary stage. The juggling analogy from the previous section is useful here again. The stage where juggling requires intense concentration and conscious effort is a real and necessary part of learning to juggle. You can't skip it. But the goal isn't to stay at that stage forever. The goal is to practice until the skill becomes more fluid, until the conscious effort gives way to something more integrated and less draining. At that point, you're not juggling with gritted teeth anymore. You're just juggling.

Regulated functioning is the stage where you're juggling with gritted teeth. And the important thing to know is that there's a stage beyond it. One where the management becomes less central, the vigilance less constant, and the internal freedom more real. Getting there doesn't require abandoning what you've built. It requires understanding why what you've built, as valuable as it is, can't be the whole answer. The control that served you at this level becomes the ceiling that limits you at the next one. Seeing that clearly is what makes it possible to move through it rather than settling for it.

Cultivating Positive Internal Resources

There's an aspect of regulated functioning that often gets overlooked in discussions about management and control. Alongside the reactive tools you use to bring difficult states down, there's a proactive dimension. The deliberate cultivation of internal resources that make you more resilient before the difficult moments arrive. This isn't about chasing happiness or forcing positivity. It's about actively building the psychological reserves that buffer against stress rather than just responding to it after the fact.

The distinction matters. Most regulation strategies are reactive by nature. Anxiety rises, you apply a technique. A negative thought spiral starts, you interrupt it. These are responses to states that have already appeared. Proactive resource cultivation works differently. It's about building something in advance, creating an internal environment that's more stable and more resilient as a baseline, so that when stressors arrive, you're not starting from empty.

Think of it as the difference between firefighting and fireproofing. Firefighting is essential when the fire is already burning. But if your entire strategy is firefighting, you're always in crisis mode, always responding, always one spark away from scrambling. Fireproofing, done consistently, changes the conditions so that the fires are less frequent and less severe when they do occur. Both matter, but most people who are working on regulated functioning are spending all their effort on firefighting and very little on fireproofing.

Gratitude practice is one of the most extensively researched proactive interventions in positive psychology. Research by Emmons and McCullough (2003) and Seligman et al. (2005) has consistently shown that regular engagement in gratitude practices is associated with increased positive affect, improved sleep quality, enhanced resilience, and stronger interpersonal relationships.

The mechanisms underlying these effects are increasingly understood. Gratitude practice appears to transformation attentional processes toward positive and meaningful aspects of experience, counteracting the well-documented human tendency toward negativity bias—the preferential attention to potential threats and adverse information (Baumeister et al., 2001). In this way, gratitude does not eliminate difficulty, but recalibrates attentional focus, allowing individuals to register resources, support, and value-relevant aspects of their environment alongside challenges.

This process can be understood as a form of attentional training. Rather than passively defaulting to threat detection—a pattern associated with reactive modes of functioning—gratitude practice actively broadens the scope of attention, supporting more flexible and adaptive engagement with experience (Fredrickson, 2001). Importantly, this is not a form of denial or avoidance; rather, it represents a deliberate rebalancing of cognitive and emotional processing in the presence of both positive and negative stimuli.

But there's a specific way to do gratitude practice that makes it genuinely useful rather than just a feel-good ritual, and most people aren't doing it that way. The key is specificity and novelty. Writing "I'm grateful for my health and my family" every day quickly becomes automatic and loses its effect. What produces genuine positive emotional response is specific, fresh, and slightly unexpected gratitude. Not "I'm grateful for my friend" but "I'm grateful for the specific thing my friend said on Tuesday that made me feel understood when I was struggling." Not "I'm grateful for my work" but "I'm grateful for the moment this morning when a problem I'd been stuck on suddenly clicked into place." The specificity forces you to actually attend to the experience rather than just labeling it. And that genuine attention is what produces the neurological and emotional effect.

Here's the exact practice. Each evening, write down three specific things from that day that you're genuinely glad happened or genuinely glad exist. They don't have to be significant. In fact, the smaller and more specific they are, the better. A good conversation. A moment of unexpected ease. Something that worked when it might not have. A physical sensation that was pleasant. A small accomplishment. Write each one as a complete sentence that includes the specific detail that made it meaningful.

Do this for thirty consecutive days. Not occasionally. Every day. The consistency is what trains the attentional transformation. After thirty days, most people report that they're noticing positive moments during the day rather than just retroactively in the evening. The practice has begun to change the real-time filter through which they experience their days.

Self-care, as a concept, has been so thoroughly commercialized that it's worth stripping it back to what it actually means in the context of building psychological resources. At its core, self-care in this context means maintaining the basic physical and relational conditions that allow your nervous system to function at its best.

Sleep, movement, nutrition, and genuine social connection aren't luxuries or rewards. They're the substrate on which everything else is built. When they're consistently compromised, your regulation capacity drops, your threshold for reactive responses lowers, and the effort required to maintain regulated functioning increases significantly. You end up working harder to achieve the same level of stability, because the foundation is unstable.

This isn't news to most people. The challenge isn't knowledge. It's the tendency to treat self-care as the first thing to cut when life gets demanding, which is precisely when it matters most. The person who stops sleeping properly during a stressful period, stops exercising because there's no time, and stops maintaining meaningful social contact because they're too busy, is systematically dismantling the internal resources they need to handle the stress they're under. The stress increases, the resources drop, the regulation becomes harder, which creates more stress, which depletes more resources. It's a spiral in the wrong direction, and it starts with the seemingly reasonable decision to prioritize output over foundation.

Building a genuine self-care structure means treating these basics as non-negotiable commitments rather than optional additions. Not because you deserve rest, though you do, but because the quality of everything else you do depends on the quality of these foundations. Sleep is the most important one.

Research by Matthew Walker at UC Berkeley has shown that *even modest sleep deprivation, defined as less than seven hours* for most adults, produces measurable impairments in emotional regulation, cognitive flexibility, and impulse control. The very capacities you're trying to build through regulated functioning get compromised by insufficient sleep more reliably than by almost any other single factor. If you're doing everything else in this book while consistently sleeping six hours or less, you're fighting uphill.

Movement is the second foundation, and it works through a direct neurological mechanism. Regular physical exercise has been shown to increase BDNF, a protein that supports the growth and maintenance of neurons, particularly in the prefrontal cortex, which is the part of your brain responsible for the deliberate, considered responses that regulated functioning requires.

Exercise also reduces baseline cortisol levels and improves sleep quality. You don't need an elaborate fitness program. You need consistent movement, ideally thirty minutes most days, at an intensity that raises your heart rate. That's the minimum effective dose for the neurological benefits that directly support your capacity to regulate.

Social connection is the third foundation, and it's the one most likely to be deprioritized by the ambitious, self-sufficient people who are most drawn to books like this one. Human beings are fundamentally social organisms. Your nervous system co-regulates with the nervous systems of people you feel safe with. Genuine connection with people you trust literally helps your nervous system settle in ways that solo regulation practices can't fully replicate.

This doesn't mean you need to be extroverted or constantly social. It means you need some relationships where you can be honest about what's actually happening for you, where you're not performing composure, where the connection is real rather than managed. Even one or two such relationships makes a measurable difference in your baseline resilience.

The proactive cultivation of these resources, gratitude practice, quality sleep, regular movement, genuine social connection, isn't a replacement for the regulation tools you've built. It's the environment in which those tools work better and cost less. When your baseline is more stable, regulation requires less effort. When regulation requires less effort, you have more capacity available for the work and relationships that actually matter to you.

And when that capacity is consistently available, you start to approach the kind of effortless functioning that transcendent operation requires. Not because you've eliminated difficulty, but because you've built a foundation robust enough that difficulty doesn't drain you the way it used to.

There's one more proactive practice worth

including here, and it's one that directly bridges regulated and transcendent functioning. This aligns with research on recovery and restoration, which shows that deliberate disengagement from stressors and reorientation toward restorative processes is essential for maintaining psychological and physiological functioning over time (Sonnentag & Fritz, 2007). Not passive rest, but the deliberate creation of mental and emotional space between periods of high demand.

This might look like a genuine lunch break where you're not consuming information or solving problems. It might look like a short walk without your phone after a difficult meeting. It might look like five minutes of deliberate stillness at the end of a demanding workday before you transition into your personal life. The content matters less than the intention. You're giving your nervous system a chance to return to baseline before the next demand arrives, rather than accumulating stress across an entire day and then wondering why you're depleted by evening.

People who build intentional recovery into their days consistently report better emotional regulation, better decision-making, and better quality of presence in their personal lives. The recovery isn't wasted time. It's maintenance on the system that makes everything else possible. And unlike the reactive regulation tools that respond to problems after they've appeared, intentional recovery prevents the accumulation that makes those problems more frequent and more severe in the first place.

Putting It Into Practice

Regulated functioning is a real and necessary stage. The skills you've built or are building here, the ability to manage emotional intensity, challenge distorted thinking, and maintain functionality under pressure, are genuine assets. They're not things to discard. They're things to understand clearly, including their costs, so you can use them wisely while continuing to build toward something more fluid.

The practices below are designed to do three specific things. First, help you identify which regulation tools you're currently using and how much they're costing you. Second, help you build the proactive resource base that makes regulation less effortful. Third, help you begin noticing the gap between managing your internal state and genuinely operating from your values, which is the gap that points toward transcendent functioning.

Practice one: Audit your current regulation toolkit. Set aside twenty minutes this week, ideally with a pen and paper. Write down every strategy you currently use to manage your internal state. Be thorough and honest. Deep breathing, journaling, reframing negative thoughts, avoiding certain situations, staying busy, exercising to burn off anxiety, talking through problems with someone, using structure and routine to feel in control. List everything.

Then, for each item on your list, write one sentence about what it costs you. Not in a judgmental way, but honestly. "This takes about ten minutes each time and leaves me feeling slightly depleted." "This works but requires me to catch the thought early, which means I'm always monitoring." "This helps but I rely on it so heavily that when I can't do it, I struggle."

The audit isn't about eliminating your tools. It's about seeing their full picture, benefits and costs together, so you can use them consciously rather than automatically.

Practice two: Start the specific gratitude practice described in this chapter. Tonight, before you sleep, write three specific things from today that you're genuinely glad happened. Each one as a complete sentence with a concrete detail. Do this every night for thirty consecutive days. If you miss a day, don't restart the count, just continue. The goal is building the habit, not maintaining a perfect streak.

After two weeks, write one sentence in your notebook about whether you're noticing positive moments during the day more readily than you were before you started. That observation is your data point. It tells you whether the attentional transformation is beginning to happen in real time.

Practice three: Identify the one foundation, sleep, movement, or social connection, that you're most consistently compromising. Just one. Don't try to fix all three at once. Pick the one that, if improved, would have the biggest impact on your baseline stability. Then make one specific, non-negotiable commitment to it for the next two weeks.

Not "I'll try to sleep more" but "I will be in bed with my phone in another room by 10:30pm on weekdays." Not "I'll exercise more" but "I will take a twenty-minute walk every day at lunch, regardless of weather or workload." Specific, bounded, and treated as a commitment rather than a preference.

After two weeks, notice whether your regulation feels different. Whether the tools cost you slightly less. Whether the baseline feels slightly more stable. That difference, even if it's small, is the fireproofing beginning to work.

Practice four: Add one intentional recovery period to each workday for the next week. Choose a consistent time, after a meeting, at the end of the morning, before you switch from work to personal time. Block five to ten minutes. During that time, do something that genuinely allows your nervous system to settle. A short walk, five minutes of deliberate stillness, a few minutes of slow breathing without an agenda. No information input, no problem-solving, no planning. Just recovery.

At the end of the week, write two sentences about what you noticed. Did your afternoons feel different? Did transitions feel less abrupt? Did you arrive at your personal time with more capacity than usual? The answers tell you whether intentional recovery is producing the effect it's designed to produce for you specifically.

Practice five: Notice the cost of control once each day. This is the most important practice in this entire section, because it's the one that points directly toward what comes next. Once each day, at any moment when you're actively managing your internal state, applying a technique, reframing a thought, using a strategy to keep yourself regulated, pause for just a few seconds and ask one question: what would it feel like to not have to manage this right now? Not to act on the difficult feeling. Not to abandon the regulation. Just to notice, briefly, what it would mean to be free from the effort of management entirely.

You're not trying to answer that question fully. You're just keeping it alive. Because that question, asked consistently, is what begins to orient you toward the next level of functioning. It points you toward the difference between managing the weather and simply being someone who can navigate it without needing to control it.

That difference is what the remaining chapters of this book are built on.

Regulated functioning is where most people

plateau. Not because they lack discipline or intelligence, but because nobody told them there was somewhere further to go. Now you know there is. The tools you've built at this level are real. The progress is real. And the next stage doesn't require you to throw any of it away. It requires you to understand it well enough to move through it, toward a way of operating that's less effortful, more free, and more fully aligned with the person you're actually capable of being.

Chapter Nine

Level 3: The Transcendent State

You've traveled a significant distance to get here. You've learned to see your thoughts as mental events rather than facts. You've built the capacity to hold difficult emotions without fleeing them. You've loosened your grip on rigid conditions and self-narratives. You've practiced acting from your values even when the internal weather wasn't cooperating. And you've seen clearly what reactive functioning costs you, and why regulated functioning, as valuable as it is, can't be the final destination.

This is the chapter where everything converges.

Level 3 isn't a reward for completing the previous work. It's what the previous work was always pointing toward. It's the state where you stop managing your internal world and start inhabiting it fully, where you stop bracing against your experience and start moving through it with genuine freedom. Not freedom from difficulty. Freedom within it. That distinction is everything, and by the end of this chapter, you'll understand exactly what it means and exactly how to access it.

The transcendent state isn't a permanent destination you arrive at and never leave. It's a way of orienting yourself that becomes more available the more you practice it. Some days you'll operate from it for hours. Other days you'll dip back into reactive or regulated modes, and that's not failure. That's being human. The difference between someone who has built this capacity and someone who hasn't isn't that the first person never gets pulled off course. It's that they know how to find their way back. Quickly. Without drama. Without the spiral of self-judgment that turns a temporary drift into a prolonged derailment.

That's what this chapter gives you. The complete picture of what transcendent functioning actually looks and feels like, why it's fundamentally different from everything that came before it, and the specific practices that make it a real, lived capacity rather than a concept you understand intellectually but can't quite reach.

Operating from a Spacious Perspective

There's a quality to transcendent functioning that's hard to describe without experiencing it, but it's worth trying. The best word for it is spaciousness. When you're operating from this level, there's a sense of room inside your experience. Room for the difficult thought to be there without it filling the whole space. Room for the uncomfortable feeling to exist without it demanding your complete attention. Room for uncertainty, for complexity, for the messy, unresolved nature of real life, without any of it collapsing you.

That spaciousness isn't emptiness. It's not detachment. It's not the numbed-out calm of someone who has suppressed everything they feel. It's the quality of a container that's large enough to hold whatever's inside it without being overwhelmed. You're the container. Your experience is what's inside. And the container doesn't become its contents.

This is the practical meaning of the self-as-context concept you encountered earlier in this book. At the reactive level, you are your emotions.

When anxiety is present, you're an anxious person. When doubt shows up, you're a doubtful person. The internal state and the self are fused. At the regulated level, you're someone who manages their emotions. Better, but the emotional state is still central. You're defined by your relationship to it, even if that relationship is now one of management rather than helplessness. At the transcendent level, you're the awareness that contains all of it. The sky, not the weather. The ocean floor, not the surface waves. Your emotions, thoughts, and sensations are events happening within your awareness. They're real. They matter. But they're not you, and they don't determine what you do next.

Think about what it actually means to operate from this position in a real situation. Suppose you're about to have a conversation you've been dreading. At the reactive level, the dread runs the show. You avoid the conversation, or you enter it so defended that genuine communication isn't possible. At the regulated level, you apply techniques before and during. You breathe. You reframe. You manage the anxiety well enough to get through it. At the transcendent level, something different happens. You notice the dread. You acknowledge it fully, without fighting it or managing it away. You recognize it as a wave moving through your awareness. And then you ask the only question that actually matters in that moment: what does the person I want to be do here? The dread is still present. It's just no longer the deciding factor.

That transformation, from internal state as decision-maker to values as decision-maker, is the operational definition of transcendent functioning. And it produces something that neither reactive nor regulated functioning can produce: genuine freedom of choice. Not freedom from feeling, but freedom within feeling. The ability to feel the full weight of your experience and still steer.

The waves and compass metaphor is worth spending time with here, because it captures something important about how this works in practice. Your emotional experience is like waves on the surface of water. They're real. They have force. They rise and fall with conditions you don't fully control. Trying to stop the waves, which is essentially what symptom management attempts, is both exhausting and ultimately futile. The waves will come. Your values are the compass. Fixed. Reliable. Pointing in a consistent direction regardless of what the surface is doing. Transcendent functioning is the practice of keeping your attention on the compass rather than being consumed by the waves. You feel the waves. You don't pretend they're not there. But you navigate by the compass.

This requires a specific kind of perspective-taking that can be practiced deliberately. When you're in the middle of a difficult experience, the natural tendency is to be completely inside it. Your attention narrows. The difficult thing fills your whole field of view. There's no room for context, for the bigger picture, for the part of you that knows this moment is one moment in a much longer story. Perspective-taking is the deliberate act of zooming out from that narrowed view to see the larger frame.

Here's a specific practice for doing this in real time. The next time you're in the middle of a challenging situation, whether it's a conflict, a setback, a spike of anxiety, or a moment of self-doubt, pause for thirty seconds and ask yourself three questions in sequence. First: what's actually happening right now, as a factual description, without the story my mind is building around it? Second: will this specific moment matter in a meaningful way one year from now? Third: what does the person I'm committed to being do in this kind of situation? These three questions don't eliminate the difficulty. They restore your access to perspective that the difficulty was temporarily blocking. The first question separates fact from narrative. The second question provides temporal context. The third question reconnects you to your values. Together, they take you from being inside the wave to being the person who can feel the wave and still hold the compass.

Practice this sequence with a current challenge you're facing right now. Not a hypothetical one. Something real that's generating genuine discomfort or uncertainty for you today. Sit with a pen and paper and write your answers to all three questions. Don't rush them. Give yourself five minutes with each one. What you're doing is practicing the perspective-taking that transcendent functioning runs on. You're training your attention to find the spacious view even when everything in you wants to stay contracted around the difficulty.

The spacious perspective also changes your relationship to time in a way that's worth naming. Reactive functioning is almost entirely present-tense. The feeling is here now, so the response is here now. Regulated functioning adds some temporal awareness, you can delay a response, apply a technique, think before reacting. But transcendent functioning has a different relationship to time entirely. It holds the present moment within a larger context. This difficult conversation is happening now, and it's also one interaction in a relationship that matters to me and that I want to build over years. This setback is real today, and it's also one event in a longer arc of work that I'm committed to regardless of any single outcome. That temporal spaciousness doesn't make the present difficulty less real. It makes it less totalizing. It gives you room to respond from your values rather than from the urgency of the immediate emotional experience.

Resilient engagement is the phrase that best captures what transcendent functioning actually looks like from the outside. Not the absence of difficulty. Not a smooth, untroubled surface. Resilient engagement. The person who keeps showing up, keeps working, keeps connecting, keeps choosing their values even when the conditions are hard. Not because they've conquered their emotions, but because their emotions have stopped having veto power over their choices. That's what people around them notice. Not that they never struggle, but that the struggle doesn't stop them. That they're present even when things are difficult. That they can be honest about what's hard without being derailed by it. That quality, that resilient engagement with life regardless of conditions, is the visible expression of the transcendent state.

Building this perspective as a genuine capacity, rather than an occasional lucky moment, requires one more specific practice. At the end of each day, for the next two weeks, take five minutes to write about one challenging moment from that day from two different perspectives. First, write about it from inside the experience, exactly how it felt in the moment, the thoughts, the feelings, the urgency. Then write about it from the spacious perspective, as if you're an observer looking at the situation with full knowledge of your values and your larger commitments.

Notice the difference between the two accounts. Notice what becomes visible from the spacious view that was invisible from inside the experience. You're not invalidating the first perspective. You're practicing the second one until it becomes more accessible in real time. That practice, done consistently for two weeks, begins to make the spacious perspective a genuine option rather than something you can only access in retrospect.

Freedom from Internal Dictation

There's a particular kind of freedom that most people have never experienced, and it's not the freedom they think they want. They think they want freedom from difficult feelings. Freedom from anxiety, from self-doubt, from the inner critic, from the fear that shows up before anything important. They want those things gone. And the promise of that kind of freedom is what sells most self-help content.

That's not the freedom this section is about.

The freedom that transcendent functioning actually delivers is something more real and more durable. It's the freedom to act from your values while difficult feelings are present. The freedom to move toward what matters without needing your internal milieu to cooperate first. The freedom to be fully human, to feel everything, and still be the one making the choices. That's freedom from internal dictation. Not freedom from internal experience, but freedom from the authority that experience has been given over your behavior.

The distinction matters because one of those

freedoms is available to you right now, and the other one isn't available to anyone, ever. You will feel fear before important things. You will feel self-doubt when you're working at the edge of your capability. You will feel grief when you lose something meaningful. You will feel anxiety when the stakes are high. These aren't design flaws. They're features of a nervous system that's working correctly. The question was never whether you'd feel them. The question is whether they get to decide what you do.

When your internal experience dictates your behavior, you're living inside a closed system. The feeling arrives. The behavior follows. The feeling is in charge. This is reactive functioning at its most basic level. Regulated functioning interrupts that chain by inserting management. The feeling arrives. You apply a technique. The feeling drops. Then you act. Better, but the feeling is still the gatekeeper. You're still waiting for the internal conditions to be acceptable before you move. The management is more sophisticated than the reaction, but the structure is the same. The internal state still runs the show, just with better tools applied to it.

Transcendent functioning breaks that structure entirely. The feeling arrives. You acknowledge it. You don't fight it, manage it away, or wait for it to drop. You feel it fully, as a real experience in your body and mind. And then you act from your values, with the feeling present. The feeling is no longer the gatekeeper. Your values are. That's the structural difference. And it's not a small one.

Consider what this means for courage specifically. Most people think of courage as something you feel. A surge of confidence, a moment of clarity, a sense of readiness that arrives and carries you forward. But that understanding of courage is actually just a description of moments when the emotional conditions happened to cooperate. Real courage, the kind that produces a consistent, reliable life, is something different. It's the capacity to act in the presence of fear, not in the absence of it. To move toward the difficult conversation, the risky creative work, the vulnerable moment, with the fear still fully present and fully felt. Not suppressed. Not managed down. Present. And not in charge.

This is one of the most practically important insights in this entire book. You don't have to wait for fear to vanish before you act. You don't have to feel confident before you begin. You don't have to feel ready before you start. The waiting for those conditions is the trap. Those conditions are unreliable, inconsistent, and frequently absent precisely when you need them most, before the things that matter most. The person who acts only when they feel ready will act rarely. The person who acts while feeling afraid, while feeling uncertain, while feeling the full weight of what's at stake, that person builds a life that actually reflects their values.

Think about a hypothetical scenario: someone like Camille, a 30-year-old writer who has been working on her first book for three years. She's talented and she knows it, but she's also been waiting. Waiting to feel more confident in her voice. Waiting until the draft is perfect enough that showing it won't feel terrifying. Waiting for the anxiety about exposure and judgment to drop to a manageable level before she lets anyone read her work. The waiting has a logic to it. The anxiety is real. But the waiting isn't protecting her from anything. It's just keeping her in place. What she hasn't understood yet is that the anxiety about sharing her work isn't a sign that she's not ready. It's a sign that the work matters to her. Fear and importance travel together. The more something matters, the more the fear shows up before it. Waiting for the fear to go away before sharing her work is the same as waiting for the work to stop mattering. That day isn't coming. The only way forward is through, with the fear present, because she values the work more than she values the comfort of not being seen.

The practical skill that makes this possible is what you might call the "feel it and move" practice. When fear, anxiety, or self-doubt shows up before something important, instead of trying to reduce it before acting, you do something specific. You acknowledge the feeling by name. You locate it in your body. You take one slow breath. And then you take the first concrete step of the action you've been avoiding, with the feeling still fully present. Not a big step. The smallest possible step that moves you toward the thing. The first sentence of the email. The first minute of the difficult conversation. The first stroke of the brush. The first line of the code. One small, real, concrete move, made with the fear present rather than after it's gone.

This practice works because it directly contradicts the structure of internal dictation. Instead of waiting for the internal conditions to change before acting, you act, and the internal conditions respond to the action rather than the other way around. What most people discover when they do this consistently is that the fear doesn't grow when you move toward it. It often peaks briefly and then begins to drop, not because you managed it, but because the action itself changes the context. You're no longer bracing against a feared future. You're in the present, doing the thing, and the present is almost always more manageable than the anticipated version of it.

Maintaining agency when your internal milieu is chaotic requires a specific kind of anchor. When everything inside you feels loud and urgent and competing for your attention, you need something stable to orient to. That anchor is your values. Not as an abstract concept, but as a concrete, specific behavioral question: given what I value, what's the next right action here? Not the perfect action. Not the action that will make the feeling go away. The next right action, aligned with who I'm committed to being. That question is always answerable, even when everything else feels unclear. And answering it, and then acting on the answer, is what agency looks like when your internal world is chaotic.

There is a second practice worth developing for moments when internal chaos is at its highest. This can be understood as a values anchor practice. When individuals are in the midst of significant emotional turbulence—such as an anxiety spike, a wave of overwhelm, a surge of self-doubt, or the paralysis that can arise when multiple difficult emotional states converge—the task is not to eliminate those experiences, but to reestablish behavioral direction through values-consistent action.

In practice, this involves three sequential steps: first, naming the internal experience without judgment; second, identifying the value most relevant to the situation; and third, taking one immediate action that reflects that value despite the presence of distress. This sequence restores agency by transformationing attention from internal chaos to chosen direction, which is a central mechanism of psychological flexibility. First, name what's happening internally without judgment: "I'm feeling anxious and overwhelmed and uncertain right now." Say it out loud if you can. The naming itself creates a small amount of distance between you and the experience. Second, identify your most relevant value for this specific situation: "What I care about most here is honesty," or "What matters most to me in this moment is showing up for the people depending on me," or "What I value here is doing work I'm genuinely proud of." Third, ask and answer the action question: "Given that value, what's one thing I can do in the next five minutes?" Then do that one thing.

This three-step sequence doesn't resolve the internal chaos. It doesn't make the difficult feelings disappear. What it does is restore your access to agency within the chaos. You're not waiting for the storm to pass before you steer. You're steering in the storm. And each time you do that, you build direct evidence that you're capable of it. That evidence accumulates. Over time, the chaotic internal states become less threatening, not because they're less intense, but because you've proven to yourself repeatedly that they don't have to stop you. You've broken the equation that says difficult internal experience equals inability to act. That equation, once broken, stays broken.

There's something worth naming about what this kind of freedom actually feels like from the inside, because it's different from what most people expect. It doesn't feel like invincibility. It doesn't feel like the absence of difficulty. It often feels quieter than that. A kind of steadiness. A sense of being present with what's hard without needing it to be different before you can move. A quality of being grounded even when you're not calm. It's not the electric confidence of a motivated day. It's something more reliable than that. It's the sense of being the person who shows up regardless, not because the feelings are gone, but because the feelings have stopped being the deciding factor. That steadiness, built through practice, is one of the most genuinely useful things a person can develop. It doesn't make life easier. It makes you more capable of living it fully, exactly as it is.

The liberation that comes from seeing thoughts and feelings as visitors rather than masters is real, but it's important to understand what that phrase actually means in practice. Visitors have presence. You notice them. You can engage with them. They can be uncomfortable or welcome. But they don't move in permanently. They don't redecorate the house to suit themselves. They don't get to determine who you are or what you do. They arrive, they're here for a while, and they pass. You remain. Your values remain. Your capacity to choose remains.

That's the practical experience of freedom from internal dictation. Not the absence of the visitors, but the clear understanding that they're visitors, not landlords.

Your Practice: Returning to What Matters

Everything in this chapter has been building toward one central understanding: transcendent functioning isn't a state you achieve once and maintain effortlessly. It's a practice of returning. Returning to your values when you've drifted from them. Returning to the spacious perspective when difficulty has pulled you into the contracted view. Returning to your agency when internal chaos has temporarily made it feel unavailable. The returning is the practice. And the quality of your life is largely determined by how quickly and how consistently you can make that return.

This is actually good news. It means the goal isn't perfection. It's not a permanent state of transcendent equanimity that you have to maintain without slipping. The goal is a practiced capacity for return. And that capacity is built through specific, repeated actions, not through insight or willpower alone.

The action steps below are built directly from everything in this chapter. They're designed to work together as a complete practice. Don't pick and choose. Work through all of them, in order, over the next three weeks.

Action step one: The three-question perspective-taking practice, applied to one current challenge today. Right now, before you move on, identify one real challenge in your life that's currently generating discomfort, anxiety, or a sense of being stuck. It doesn't have to be dramatic. It just has to be real. Write your answers to the three questions from the first section: what's actually happening as a factual description without the story your mind is building around it? Will this specific moment matter meaningfully one year from now? What does the person you're committed to being do in this kind of situation?

Write full answers, not quick notes. Give each question at least three minutes. When you're done, write one sentence describing the action that the third question points you toward. That sentence is your next move on this challenge. Take that action today, not tomorrow. The practice only works when it connects to real behavior in your actual life.

Action step two: The daily two-perspective writing practice for fourteen consecutive days. Each evening, identify one challenging moment from that day. Write two short paragraphs about it. The first paragraph from inside the experience, exactly how it felt, the thoughts, the feelings, the urgency, the difficulty. The second paragraph from the spacious perspective, as if you're looking at the situation with full access to your values and your larger commitments. Keep each paragraph to five to eight sentences.

This isn't a journaling exercise about processing your feelings. It's a deliberate training practice for the spacious view. You're building the neural pathway that makes perspective-taking accessible in real time rather than only available in retrospect. After fourteen days, read back through both columns of entries. Notice how the spacious perspective changes what you see about each situation. Notice which values kept appearing in the second paragraphs. Those recurring values are telling you something important about what your compass actually points toward.

Action step three: The "feel it and move" practice, applied to one avoided action this week. Identify one thing you've been putting off because the feelings around it are uncomfortable. Be specific. Not "I've been avoiding difficult work" but "I've been avoiding sending the email to [specific person] about [specific thing] because I feel anxious about how they'll respond." Once you have the specific avoided action named, schedule a ten-minute block in the next forty-eight hours.

When that block arrives, acknowledge the feeling by name, locate it in your body, take one slow breath, and take the smallest possible concrete first step of the avoided action. One sentence of the email. One minute of the difficult conversation. One small, real move. With the feeling present. Don't wait for the feeling to drop first. Do it with the feeling there. After you've done it, write one sentence about what you noticed. Did the feeling grow or peak and then drop? Did the action feel more manageable once you were in it than it did in anticipation? That sentence is your evidence. It goes into the same notebook as your two-perspective entries.

Over time, that notebook becomes a record of your own demonstrated capacity to act in the presence of difficult feelings. That record is more motivating than any amount of theoretical understanding.

Action step four: The values anchor practice, used at least once in the next seven days during a moment of genuine internal chaos. You don't need to manufacture a difficult moment for this. Life will provide one. When it does, and when you notice that your internal milieu is chaotic enough that your agency feels temporarily unavailable, run the three-step sequence. Name what's happening internally without judgment. Identify your most relevant value for this specific situation. Ask and answer the action question: given that value, what's one thing I can do in the next five minutes? Then do it.

After the moment has passed, write down what happened. What was the internal state? What value did you identify? What action did you take? What was the result? This written record matters because it builds your evidence base. Each entry is proof that you can maintain agency in chaos. And that proof, accumulated over weeks and months, changes your relationship to chaos itself. It stops being something that shuts you down and starts being something you know how to navigate.

Action step five: A weekly five-minute reflection on the practice of returning. Every Sunday, set a timer for five minutes and answer three questions in writing. Where did I drift from my values this week, and what pulled me there? Where did I successfully return to my values after drifting, and what made that return possible? What's one specific thing I'll do differently this coming week based on what I noticed? These three questions aren't about self-criticism. They're about building the metacognitive awareness that makes transcendent functioning more consistent over time.

The person who reviews their week honestly and identifies specific patterns learns from their experience. The person who moves through their weeks without reflection repeats the same patterns indefinitely. Five minutes, every Sunday, in writing. That's the practice. It's small enough to actually do and significant enough to produce real change over months.

Transcendent functioning is the apex of the model this book has been building, but it's not a fixed peak you reach and stand on permanently. It's a direction. A way of orienting yourself that becomes more natural the more you practice it.

The waves of emotion will keep coming. The difficult thoughts will keep arriving. The fear will keep showing up before the things that matter most. None of that changes. What changes is your relationship to all of it. You stop being someone who is managed by their internal experience and become someone who can feel everything and still choose. That's not a small transformation. It's the transformation that makes everything else in your life more possible. And it's available to you right now, through conscious choice, exactly as things are.

Chapter Ten

Authentic Engagement: Living with Aliveness

Something transformations when you stop spending your energy fighting yourself. It's subtle at first. You notice it in small moments. A conversation that actually lands instead of skimming the surface. A piece of work that feels genuinely satisfying rather than just completed. A quiet Tuesday afternoon that feels, unexpectedly, like enough. These aren't dramatic revelations. They're the natural result of what happens when the internal war winds down and your attention is finally free to go somewhere else.

That's what this chapter is about.

The previous chapters built a specific architecture. Defusion created distance from your thoughts. Experiential expansion widened your capacity to hold difficult feelings. Attachment reduction loosened the grip of rigid conditions and self-narratives. Intentional action gave you a working system for moving toward your values regardless of your emotional state. And Chapters 7, 8, and 9 mapped the three levels of functioning so you could see exactly where you've been operating and what the next level actually requires.

All of that was preparation. This chapter is about what you get to do with it.

When you're no longer primarily organized around avoiding discomfort, when your execution doesn't depend on your emotional state cooperating, when your identity isn't threatened every time life doesn't go according to plan, something opens up. The energy that was tied up in management becomes available. The attention that was locked on internal monitoring gets redirected outward. And what you find there, in the world that your defended self had been only partially inhabiting, is richer than you expected. More textured. More alive. More worth showing up for.

That aliveness isn't a mood. It's not a peak state you chase. It's what authentic engagement with your actual life feels like when the noise goes quiet enough to let it through.

Savoring Life's Richness

Most people are consuming their lives rather than tasting them.

They move through experiences the way you scroll through a feed. Fast, continuous, half-attentive. The meal is eaten while checking the phone. The conversation is happening while planning the response. The walk outside is spent rehearsing tomorrow's difficult meeting. The moment is always slightly elsewhere, always filtered through the background hum of what needs to be managed, fixed, avoided, or prepared for. Life is technically happening. But the full experience of it isn't getting through.

This isn't laziness or ingratitude. It's the inevitable result of a nervous system that's been running in threat-detection mode for too long. When your primary psychological project has been managing your internal state, your attention narrows. It focuses on what's wrong, what might go wrong, and what needs to be done about it. That narrowed focus is useful in genuine emergencies. As a permanent operating mode, it filters out most of what makes being alive actually worth something.

Savoring is the deliberate practice of reversing that filter. It is the conscious act of allowing a positive or meaningful experience to fully register —to be noticed, sustained, and integrated—rather than passing through awareness on the way to the next demand. This process involves intentionally attending to and enhancing positive experience in the present moment.

Research on savoring demonstrates that the capacity to savor positive experiences is a distinct psychological skill, one that is relatively independent of the frequency of positive events themselves and can be deliberately cultivated. Individuals who are more effective at savoring tend to experience greater well-being not because they encounter more positive events, but because they engage with those events more fully and for longer durations.The frequency of positive events in your life matters less than your capacity to actually receive them when they occur.

Think about what savoring actually requires. It requires presence. You can't savor something you're not fully in. It requires a certain willingness to let something be good without immediately hedging it with worry about when it will end. It requires, in a very real sense, the absence of the defensive posture that reactive and regulated functioning maintain almost constantly. You can't be braced and open at the same time. The spaciousness that transcendent functioning creates isn't just useful for navigating difficulty. It's what makes genuine pleasure, genuine beauty, and genuine satisfaction actually accessible.

Consider a hypothetical scenario: someone like Mei, a 28-year-old architect who has spent most of her adult life in high-achievement mode. She's accomplished a great deal. She's also, she admits, rarely actually enjoyed any of it. The project completion is immediately replaced by the next project. The good feedback is noted and filed. The weekend trip she planned for months is spent partly thinking about Monday. She's not depressed. She's not even particularly anxious. She's just never quite there for her own life. The experiences are happening to her, but she's not fully inside them. What she's missing isn't more positive experiences. She has plenty. What she's missing is the capacity to actually receive them.

Savoring isn’t passive. It is an active practice with specific techniques that produce measurable effects on well-being. Bryant's research identified several concrete savoring behaviors that consistently amplify positive experience.

The first is sensory absorption, which involves deliberately directing attention to the physical details of a positive experience. The specific warmth of sunlight on your face. The exact flavor of something you're eating. The particular quality of a sound you enjoy. The physical sensation of a good conversation landing. These details are always available—most of the time, attention is elsewhere. Sensory absorption is the practice of bringing attention back to immediate experience, a process consistent with research on attentional engagement and emotional amplification.

The second savoring behavior is sharing. Positive experiences are amplified when they are communicated to someone else. Not posted online for validation, but genuinely shared with a person you care about. Telling someone about something that moved you, describing it in specific detail, and reliving it through the telling extends the experience and deepens its emotional impact. Research consistently shows that sharing positive experiences with others predicts increased well-being, partly through strengthening social connection and partly through reinforcing emotional and cognitive processing of the event.

The third savoring behavior is what Bryant calls "memory building," which involves deliberately creating a mental snapshot of a moment you want to remember. Pausing in the middle of a positive experience and consciously noting: this is one I want to keep. What does it look, feel, smell, and sound like right now? This is not nostalgia—it is intentional presence. Rather than leaving the moment to preserve it, attention is deepened while the experience is still unfolding, which supports encoding and retention of positive experiences.

Here is a simple savoring practice. Once each day, for the next two weeks, identify one experience with some positive quality. It does not have to be significant—a good cup of coffee, a moment of genuine laughter, a piece of work you feel good about, or a brief interaction that felt real. When you notice it, pause for sixty seconds. Direct your full attention to the sensory details of the experience and identify at least three specific aspects of it. Then, later in the day, share it with one person directly. This sequence—absorption, articulation, and sharing—trains attentional engagement with positive experience and strengthens its emotional impact.

There is a deeper dimension to savoring that connects to the broader framework of this book. When internal demands for control and vigilance are reduced, attentional resources become more available for processing external experience. As a result, ordinary experiences can feel qualitatively different—not because the environment has changed, but because attention is no longer dominated by internal monitoring. Research on attentional load and emotional processing suggests that reduced threat-related activation allows for broader and more detailed sensory and cognitive processing.

This is not mystical—it reflects how attentional and emotional systems operate. When threat-related processing is reduced, perceptual and experiential access expands. The world does not change—your access to it does.

That access is one of the most practical outcomes of the processes developed throughout this book. The sense of aliveness that emerges is not something that must be created—it is what becomes available when competing demands on attention and processing are reduced.

Deepening Connection and Intimacy

One of the quietest costs of chronic self-management is what it does to your relationships.

When a significant portion of your attention is directed inward, monitoring your internal state, managing your reactions, maintaining the performance of composure, you're not fully present with the people in front of you. You're there, but you're also partly elsewhere. And people feel that. Not always consciously, not always articulately, but they feel the quality of your attention. They feel whether you're actually listening or just waiting for your turn to speak. They feel whether you're genuinely curious about their experience or processing it through the filter of your own concerns. They feel the difference between being seen and being managed.

Genuine connection requires something that management mode can't provide: real presence. The kind of attention that's fully available to another person because it's not simultaneously occupied with your own internal weather report.

This is one of the most significant and least-discussed benefits of transcendent functioning. When you are no longer primarily organized around your own internal experience, you develop what might be called relational bandwidth—the capacity to attend to another person's experience with reduced self-referential filtering. This includes the ability to listen without simultaneously planning a response, to remain present without redirecting the interaction toward one's own experience, and to tolerate another person's distress without immediately attempting to fix or minimize it. These capacities are closely related to constructs such as empathic accuracy, presence, and attentional control, which have been shown to improve interpersonal functioning.

The transformation from experiencing others primarily in terms of one's own needs to recognizing them as distinct individuals with independent inner lives represents a meaningful change in relational processing. When functioning reactively, other people are often perceived in terms of their relevance to one's own internal state —sources of threat, validation, comfort, or irritation. This aligns with research on self-referential processing, which shows that internal concerns can dominate perception and interpretation of social information.

At more regulated levels of functioning, individuals become aware of this tendency and begin to modulate their responses. However, attention may still be partially occupied with managing internal reactions. At more advanced levels of functioning, attentional resources can be more fully directed outward, allowing for genuine curiosity about another person's experience. This form of engagement—characterized by openness, non-defensiveness, and sustained attention—is strongly associated with perceived intimacy and relational satisfaction.

Consider what it feels like to be on the receiving end of that kind of attention. When someone is fully present—tracking what you are saying, responding without preoccupation, and engaging without defensiveness—the quality of the interaction changes. Research on perceived responsiveness shows that when individuals feel understood, validated, and cared for, they experience increased trust, emotional safety, and relational closeness. This often leads to greater openness, clearer thinking, and reduced self-monitoring during interaction.

The experience of being genuinely received by another person is one of the most psychologically nourishing forms of human connection. Importantly, this form of connection depends not on technique, but on the availability of attentional and emotional resources. It becomes possible when individuals are less preoccupied with managing their own internal states and more able to engage directly with the experience of another.c practice for deepening connection is what might be called presence-based listening. It is different from active listening in the conventional sense. Active listening is a technique; presence-based listening is a state. It reflects the ability to sustain attention on another person with reduced self-referential interference, a capacity closely related to mindfulness and attentional control .

Here is how to practice it in a real conversation. Before the conversation begins, take one slow breath and set a single intention: to be curious about this person's actual experience rather than focused on your own. During the conversation, notice when your attention drifts—to your own thoughts, your planned response, your evaluation of what they are saying, or your internal state. When you notice this, gently redirect attention back to them. Not to what you think they mean, but to what they are actually saying. This process of noticing and redirecting attention reflects core mechanisms of psychological flexibility and attentional regulation.

Ask one question that follows directly from something they said—not a question prepared in advance, but one that could only arise from having attended to that specific moment. After the conversation, notice what you learned about this person that you did not know before. If you cannot answer that question, your attention was likely directed more toward your own internal experience than toward theirs.

Do this practice with one person today. A conversation that is already going to happen, not a manufactured one. Your partner, a colleague, a friend. Set the intention beforehand. Notice where your attention goes. Ask one genuine follow-up question. That is the complete practice. It requires no additional time—only a transformation in attentional quality. Research on perceived responsiveness suggests that even small increases in attentive presence can have immediate effects on how others experience an interaction, increasing feelings of understanding, validation, and connection.

There is a specific obstacle to genuine

connection that is worth naming directly, particularly among individuals who have engaged in significant psychological work: the tendency to process other people's experiences through one's own interpretive framework. This can lead to analyzing, reframing, or attempting to explain another person's experience in real time. While this may feel like engagement from the inside, it can be experienced by others as distancing or evaluative rather than connecting. This reflects a form of self-referential processing, where attention remains anchored in one's own cognitive framework rather than fully engaging with external experience.

Genuine intimacy does not require complete understanding—it requires presence. These are distinct processes. Understanding involves interpretation; presence involves sustained attention without immediate evaluation. Research on empathy and interpersonal attunement suggests that the latter is often more strongly associated with feelings of closeness and relational safety (Davis, 1983; Reis & Shaver, 1988).

The deeper principle is that authentic engagement with others requires genuine interest in their experience as it is—not as it should be, not as it relates to one's own experience, and not as a problem to be solved. This form of attention, characterized by openness and reduced defensiveness, allows individuals to feel known rather than merely interacted with. Over time, this pattern of interaction supports the development of stable, resilient connections, which are central to psychological well-being and functioning (Reis et al., 2004).

Intrinsic Motivation and Passionate Pursuit

There's a version of ambition that's driven by fear, and most high-achieving people know it from the inside even if they've never named it that way. The fear of falling behind. The fear of not being enough. The fear of what it would mean if the project fails, if the idea doesn't land, if the effort turns out to have been insufficient. This kind of ambition produces real output. It can drive impressive results. But it's exhausting in a way that compounds over time, because the engine running it is anxiety, and anxiety is not a renewable resource.

When your motivation is primarily organized

around avoiding a feared outcome, you're always one failure away from the whole system collapsing. The work feels urgent rather than meaningful. The accomplishments feel like relief rather than satisfaction. The next goal appears before the current one has been properly received. And the question that follows you through everything, the question you're trying to outrun with every achievement, never quite gets answered, because no external result can permanently settle an internal question.

Intrinsic motivation works differently. It's driven not by what you're trying to avoid but by what you genuinely care about. The value of the work itself. The quality of engagement it produces. The sense of expressing something that matters to you through the doing of it. Research by Edward Deci and Richard Ryan at the University of Rochester, who developed Self-Determination Theory over several decades, has consistently found that intrinsic motivation produces better sustained performance, greater creativity, more resilience in the face of setbacks, and higher wellbeing than extrinsic motivation. The difference isn't marginal. It's significant and it's durable.

The connection between value-alignment and

intrinsic motivation is direct. When what you're working on is genuinely connected to something you care about, the work itself becomes a source of meaning rather than just a means to an end. The process has value independent of the outcome. This doesn't mean the outcome stops mattering. It means the outcome is no longer the only thing that makes the effort worthwhile. And that transformation changes your relationship to difficulty within the work entirely. Setbacks are information rather than verdicts. Slow progress is part of the process rather than evidence of failure. The hard days are still hard, but they're hard in the way that meaningful things are hard, not in the way that pointless things are hard.

Think about the difference between two people working on the same project. The first person is working on it because it's expected of them, because the outcome will prove something, or because the alternative feels worse. The second person is working on it because it's genuinely connected to something they value, because the doing of it expresses something real about who they are and what they care about. When the project hits a difficult stretch, which it will, the first person's motivation collapses. The fuel was external, and the external conditions have turned unfavorable. The second person's motivation transformations but doesn't disappear. It draws from something the difficult stretch can't touch: the value underneath the work.

Here's how to build a more direct connection between your current work and your genuine values, using a practice that takes about fifteen minutes and produces something immediately useful. Take a piece of paper and write down one project or commitment that's currently part of your life, something you're working on or should be working on. Underneath it, write your honest answer to this question: why does this matter to me, separate from any external reward or consequence? Don't settle for the first answer your mind produces. Go deeper. Ask "and why does that matter?" at least three times. What you're looking for is the value underneath the goal, the thing that would make the work worth doing even if nobody ever noticed or rewarded you for it. Once you find it, write it as a single clear sentence: "This work matters to me because it expresses my value of [specific value]." Post that sentence somewhere you'll see it when the work gets hard. Not as a motivational poster. As a factual reminder of why you chose this in the first place.

The practical effect of this connection is significant. When you're having a difficult day with a project and you can reconnect to the genuine value underneath it, the difficulty changes character. It's no longer a sign that you should stop. It's the texture of doing something that matters. Resistance and meaning often travel together. The things worth doing are frequently the things that feel hardest to start and most tempting to abandon. Value-alignment doesn't eliminate that resistance. It gives you a reason to stay with it that's more durable than motivation or willpower.

There's a specific quality of engagement that emerges when intrinsic motivation is running the show, and it's worth describing concretely because it's something you may have experienced in glimpses without knowing what it was. Psychologist Mihaly Csikszentmihalyi called it flow: the state of complete absorption in a challenging activity where self-consciousness drops away, time distorts, and the doing itself becomes its own reward.

Flow isn't something you can force. But you can create the conditions for it. It tends to appear when the challenge level of the task is well-matched to your skill level, when you have clear goals for what you're doing, and when you're not simultaneously monitoring your internal state or performing for an audience. All three of those conditions are more available when you're operating from transcendent functioning, because the self-monitoring drops. The performance anxiety quiets. The values-connection provides the clear goal. And the work has room to become absorbing rather than just effortful.

The passionate pursuit of goals from a place of value-alignment rather than fear-avoidance also changes how you handle the inevitable failures and setbacks. When your sense of self is tied to a specific outcome, a setback threatens your identity. You're not just failing at the thing. You're becoming the kind of person who fails. That's an enormous psychological stake to attach to any single result, and it makes the fear of failure disproportionately large relative to what failure actually costs. When your sense of self is anchored in your values rather than your outcomes, a setback is just a setback. The project didn't work. The pitch didn't land. The plan needs to change. These are real disappointments, and they deserve to be felt as such. But they don't threaten who you are, because who you are isn't defined by any particular result. It's expressed through the quality of engagement you bring to your work, and that quality is available regardless of how any specific outcome turns out.

That's the animating force that transcendent functioning makes possible. Not the frantic energy of someone running from failure, but the sustained, grounded energy of someone moving toward something real. It doesn't burn out the same way. It doesn't require constant external reinforcement to stay alive. It's renewable in a way that fear-based motivation fundamentally isn't, because it draws from something that doesn't deplete when conditions get hard. It draws from what you actually value. And that source doesn't run dry.Putting It Into Practice

This chapter has covered three distinct but deeply connected dimensions of authentic engagement: the capacity to actually receive your own life through savoring, the capacity to genuinely meet other people through presence-based connection, and the capacity to work from intrinsic motivation rather than fear-driven urgency. Each one is a direct expression of what transcendent functioning actually produces when it's lived rather than just understood.

The practices below are your concrete steps

forward. They're specific, they're actionable, and each one has a clear outcome you can verify. Work through them in order over the next two weeks.

Step one: The daily savoring practice, starting today. Once each day, identify one experience with some positive quality to it. Stop for sixty seconds. Direct your full attention to three specific sensory details of the experience. Later that day, tell one specific person about it in a direct communication. Do this every single day for fourteen days. After the fourteen days, write three sentences about what you noticed. Did you start catching positive moments earlier in the day? Did the quality of your attention during ordinary experiences change at all? Did sharing them change how you experienced the conversations where you shared them? Those three sentences are your data. They tell you whether the attentional transformation is happening in your actual daily life.

Step two: One presence-based conversation today. Before the conversation begins, take one breath and set the intention to be genuinely curious about this person's actual experience. During the conversation, notice when your attention drifts to your own thoughts or planned responses and bring it back to them. Ask one question that could only be asked because you were listening to what they specifically said. After the conversation, write one sentence about what you learned about this person that you didn't know before. If you can't answer that, repeat the practice tomorrow with someone else. Keep going until you can answer it. That answer is the evidence that genuine presence happened rather than managed interaction.

Step three: The value-underneath exercise for one current project. Pick one project or commitment that's currently part of your life. Write down your honest answer to "why does this matter to me, separate from any external reward?" Ask "and why does that matter?" at least three times to get beneath the surface answer. Write the final answer as a single sentence in the format: "This work matters to me because it expresses my value of [specific value]." Post that sentence somewhere visible in your workspace. The next time the work gets difficult, read it before deciding whether to continue or step away. Notice whether the difficulty feels different when you're connected to the value underneath it versus when you're just responding to the discomfort of the hard stretch.

Step four: A weekly aliveness check-in. Every

Sunday for the next four weeks, spend five minutes answering these three questions in writing. Where did I feel most genuinely alive and present this week, and what was happening in those moments? Where did I feel most disconnected or like I was going through motions? Based on those two answers, what's one specific thing I'll prioritize or do differently this coming week? This isn't a gratitude journal. It's a calibration practice. You're using your own lived experience as feedback about how closely your daily life is aligned with the kind of authentic engagement this chapter describes. Over four weeks, patterns will emerge. The patterns tell you where your attention and energy are actually going versus where you want them to go. That information is more useful than any amount of abstract self-knowledge.

Aliveness isn't something you add to your life. It's what's already there when the defenses come down, when the management quiets, when your attention is finally free to be where you actually are. The work of the previous eight chapters cleared the ground for this. These practices are how you learn to stand on it.

The Role of Self-Compassion in

Growth

There's a pattern that shows up reliably in people who are doing serious work on themselves. They learn the tools. They understand the concepts. They can explain cognitive defusion, experiential expansion, attachment reduction, and intentional action with real clarity. And then they have a hard week. They drift from their values. They react when they meant to respond. They miss the practice they committed to, or they show up for it badly, or they watch themselves fall back into exactly the pattern they thought they'd moved past.

And then they turn on themselves, but not dramatically. Not usually. Not with obvious self-loathing. It's subtler than that. A quiet verdict. A tightening. The inner voice that says: you know better than this. You've read the chapters. You've done the exercises. And here you are again. The criticism feels like accountability. It feels like the appropriate response to falling short. But it isn't. And understanding why it isn't, and what to replace it with, is one of the most practically important things this book can give you.

Self-compassion isn't the soft option. It's not a way of letting yourself off the hook or lowering your standards. The research on this is clear and consistent: people who treat themselves with compassion after setbacks are more likely to try again, more likely to learn from what went wrong, and more likely to sustain meaningful change over time. The harsh inner critic doesn't produce better performance. It produces shame, avoidance, and the kind of all-or-nothing thinking that turns one difficult week into a reason to abandon everything you've built.

This chapter is about building the internal environment that makes genuine, sustained growth possible. Not just the tools for growth, but the conditions under which those tools can actually work.

The Gentle Support System

Think about the conditions under which you learn best. Not the conditions that produce the most short-term output, but the ones where genuine development actually happens. Where you're willing to try things you might get wrong. Where a mistake becomes information rather than a verdict. Where you can look honestly at what isn't working without it threatening your entire sense of who you are. Those conditions almost never involve a harsh, punishing inner environment. They involve something closer to the opposite.

The relationship between self-criticism and growth is one of the most misunderstood dynamics in personal development. The intuition most people carry is that being hard on yourself keeps you sharp. That compassion is for people who aren't serious about improving. That if you go easy on yourself after a failure, you'll stop caring about the failure. This intuition is understandable. It's also consistently wrong.

Kristin Neff at the University of Texas has spent over two decades studying self-compassion, and her findings challenge this intuition directly.

People who score high on self-compassion show greater motivation to improve after failure, not less. They're more willing to acknowledge their mistakes honestly, because acknowledging a mistake doesn't threaten their fundamental sense of worth. They take more risks, because a potential failure isn't catastrophic to their self-concept. They persist longer through difficulty, because the difficulty doesn't come packaged with a running commentary about what it means about them as a person. The self-compassionate person isn't less serious about growth. They're actually better positioned for it.

The reason connects directly to everything you've built in the previous chapters. Harsh self-criticism is itself a form of experiential avoidance. When you punish yourself for a failure, you're not actually processing the failure. You're generating a secondary experience, the shame and self-attack, that drowns out the information the failure was carrying. The self-criticism feels like engagement with the problem. Often it's a way of not having to sit with the simpler, cleaner discomfort of having gotten something wrong and needing to learn from it. The punishment substitutes for the learning.

Self-compassion creates a different internal

environment entirely. One where you can look at what happened without the looking being a threat. Where the honest acknowledgment of a mistake doesn't spiral into a verdict on your character. Where you can ask "what got in the way and what would I do differently?" without those questions triggering a shame response that shuts down your capacity to actually answer them. That environment, the one where honest self-examination is safe, is the only environment where real learning happens.

Creating that environment isn't passive. It's an active, practiced skill. And it starts with understanding what self-compassion actually consists of, because the word gets used loosely in ways that strip it of its real meaning.

Neff's model identifies three components. The first is *self-kindness*, which means treating yourself with the same basic decency you'd offer a person you care about who was struggling. Not excessive indulgence. Not making excuses. Just the absence of cruelty. When a friend comes to you having made a mistake, you don't typically say: you should have known better. You've done this before. What's wrong with you? You offer something more useful. You acknowledge what happened, you help them understand it, and you express confidence in their ability to move forward. Self-kindness is the practice of offering yourself that same quality of response.

The second component is *mindfulness* of painful experiences. This means acknowledging difficult feelings without suppressing them or getting swept away by them. It's the middle path between the two extremes people typically fall into after a setback: either numbing out and pretending it didn't matter, or catastrophizing and letting it consume everything. Mindful acknowledgment says: this is hard. I'm feeling disappointed and frustrated. I can hold that without it taking over.

The third component is *common humanity*, and it deserves its own section because it's the one that most directly addresses the particular kind of suffering that ambitious, self-aware people experience most acutely.

Here's your specific practice for building the internal support system. When you notice harsh self-criticism arising, whether after a setback, a drift from your values, or a moment where you acted in ways you're not proud of, use this three-step sequence. *First, name what happened in plain language without drama:* "I got reactive in that conversation" or "I avoided the work I said I'd do this week." Just the fact, stated clearly. *Second, offer yourself one sentence of honest acknowledgment that includes both the difficulty and the basic decency:* "That was harder than I handled it well, and that's genuinely okay to struggle with." *Third, ask the question that makes the experience useful:* "What's one thing I can take from this that helps me do it differently next time?" Write the answer down. The writing matters. It converts the self-critical spiral into something that actually produces information.

Do this sequence every time you notice harsh self-judgment arising over the next two weeks. Not occasionally. Every time. What you're building is a new default response to your own imperfection. One that's honest without being punishing. One that takes the failure seriously without making it mean something permanent about you. That response, practiced consistently, changes the internal environment in which all the other work in this book happens. It makes the work sustainable in a way that self-criticism never can.

Common Humanity and Emotional Safety

There's a specific quality to the suffering that comes after a setback when you're working seriously on yourself. It's not just the pain of the setback itself. It's the additional layer of isolation. The sense that everyone else is managing this better than you are. That other people don't struggle this much with the things you struggle with. That your particular messiness, your specific inconsistencies, your recurring patterns, are somehow more embarrassing or more fundamental than what other people deal with. You're not just failing. You're failing in a way that sets you apart.

That sense of isolation is almost always false. But it's remarkably persistent, and it does real damage.

Common humanity is the understanding that struggle, imperfection, failure, and the experience of falling short of your own standards are not exceptional conditions. They're the ordinary texture of human experience. Not for some people. For all people. The person who looks like they have it together is managing their own version of the same fundamental challenges. The high-performer you compare yourself to has their own recurring patterns, their own difficult weeks, their own gap between who they're trying to be and how they actually showed up on a given day. The difference isn't that they don't struggle. The difference is usually just what their particular struggle looks like and whether they talk about it.

This isn't a consolation prize. It's a genuine psychological transformation with real consequences for how you process difficulty. When you experience your struggle as isolating, you add the weight of separateness to whatever you're already carrying. You're not just dealing with the setback. You're dealing with the setback plus the shame of being uniquely deficient. When you recognize your struggle as part of shared human experience, the weight changes. The setback is still real. But it's no longer evidence that something is fundamentally wrong with you specifically. It's evidence that you're a human being working on something difficult. That's a different experience entirely.

Consider a hypothetical scenario: someone like James, a 37-year-old entrepreneur who has been working hard on his own functioning for about two years. He's made real progress. He's more consistent than he used to be. He handles pressure better. He's less reactive in difficult conversations. And then he has a month where everything seems to slide backward. He snaps at his team twice in one week. He avoids a financial conversation he knows he needs to have. He stops his morning practice, tells himself he'll restart Monday, and Monday keeps moving. The setback itself is real, but what James finds most painful is the story he builds around it. That he should be past this by now. That two years of work should mean he doesn't still struggle like this. That something must be fundamentally wrong with his capacity for growth if he keeps returning to the same patterns. That story, the one about being uniquely deficient, is what makes the month genuinely crushing rather than just difficult.

What James doesn't have access to in those moments is the recognition that every person doing serious growth work has months like this. That the pattern of progress followed by regression followed by return is not a sign of failure. It's the actual shape of how human beings change. The research on behavior change consistently shows that it's not linear. People don't improve in a straight upward line. They improve in a spiral, returning to old patterns, but each time from a slightly different position, with slightly more awareness, with slightly better tools for the return. The regression isn't evidence that the growth wasn't real. It's part of the process by which the growth becomes durable.

Common humanity gives James a different story to tell about his difficult month. Not a story that excuses the reactive moments or minimizes the avoidance. But a story that places those things in an accurate context. He struggled. People doing this work struggle. The struggling doesn't define the trajectory. The return does. And the return is more available, more likely, and less effortful when the story around the struggle isn't one of unique deficiency.

Compassionate self-talk is the practical skill that makes common humanity more than just an idea. It's the specific language you use internally when things go wrong. Most people have never examined the language of their inner critic. They've just lived inside it for so long that it feels like their own voice rather than a learned pattern.

Bringing conscious attention to that language, and deliberately replacing it with something more accurate and more useful, is one of the highest-leverage practices in this entire book.

Here's how to do this concretely. For the next week, pay attention to the specific sentences your inner critic produces after a setback or a moment of falling short. Write them down exactly as they appear. Not a paraphrase. The actual words. "You always do this." "You should be better than this by now." "Everyone else manages to hold it together." "What's the point of all this work if you keep ending up here?" Write them down without judgment. You're collecting data, not performing self-flagellation.

Then, for each sentence, write a response that does three things: acknowledges what actually happened, places it in the context of common humanity, and points toward the next useful move. So "you always do this" becomes: "I did this again, and that's genuinely frustrating. Struggling with this particular pattern is something a lot of people working on growth deal with. What's one thing I can do differently in the next similar situation?" The response isn't cheerful. It doesn't pretend the setback didn't happen. It's honest, grounded, and forward-pointing. That's the quality of self-talk that actually produces better behavior rather than just more suffering.

There's a specific phrase that's worth building into your vocabulary for difficult moments. When you notice yourself in the middle of a struggle, whether it's an emotional spiral, a moment of reactive behavior, or the particular exhaustion of a week where nothing seemed to go right, say this to yourself: "This is part of it." Not "this is fine" or "this doesn't matter." Just: this is part of it. Part of being human. Part of doing work that's genuinely hard. Part of the process by which real change happens. That phrase does something specific. It places the current difficulty inside a larger context without minimizing it. It reminds you that you're not uniquely broken. And it keeps the door open for the return, which is always the move that matters most.

Emotional safety is the condition that common humanity and self-compassion together create. It's the internal environment where you can be honest about what's happening without that honesty being a threat. Where you can acknowledge a failure without it becoming a verdict. Where you can see your own patterns clearly without the seeing being an act of self-punishment. That safety isn't softness. It's the foundation on which genuine accountability becomes possible. You can only look at something honestly when looking at it doesn't feel dangerous. Self-compassion makes the looking safe. And safe looking is what produces real learning, real change, and real growth over time.

The connection back to the broader model is direct. Transcendent functioning, operating above your emotions rather than being managed by them, requires a stable internal foundation. Not a perfect one. Not an untroubled one. But one that doesn't collapse every time things go wrong. Self-compassion is what builds that foundation. The person who meets their own setbacks with curiosity rather than condemnation, with honesty rather than either denial or catastrophizing, with the recognition that struggle is shared rather than shameful, that person has a foundation that holds. And a foundation that holds is what makes everything else in this book sustainable rather than just temporary.

Recap and Action Steps

Self-compassion is not a supplement to the work of transcendent functioning. It's the internal climate in which that work either flourishes or withers. Without it, the tools from every previous chapter become weapons you use against yourself when you fail to use them perfectly. With it, those tools become genuinely useful instruments for ongoing growth, because failure to use them perfectly becomes information rather than evidence of your inadequacy.

The core ideas from this chapter are worth stating plainly before you move into the action steps. Harsh self-criticism doesn't produce better performance. It produces shame, avoidance, and the kind of thinking that turns temporary setbacks into reasons to abandon progress. Self-compassion, practiced consistently, produces the internal environment where honest self-examination is possible, where learning from failure actually happens, and where the return to your values after drifting is quicker and less dramatic. Common humanity, the recognition that struggle and imperfection are shared rather than isolating, removes the additional weight of separateness from whatever difficulty you're already carrying. Compassionate self-talk replaces the inner critic's verdicts with language that's honest, grounded, and forward-pointing. And emotional safety, the condition that all of this creates, is what makes genuine accountability possible rather than just painful.

These ideas aren't just conceptually important. They're practically urgent for anyone who has been using self-criticism as a primary accountability strategy and wondering why the strategy keeps producing the same cycle of brief improvement followed by collapse.

The action steps below are specific. Each one has a clear, observable outcome. Work through them in the order they're given.

Action step one: Today, identify one self-critical thought that has appeared repeatedly over the past month. Be precise. Not "I'm too hard on myself" but the actual sentence your inner critic produces. Write it down exactly. Then, directly underneath it, write a response using the three-part structure from this chapter: acknowledge what actually happened, place it in the context of common humanity using the phrase "this is something many people working on growth deal with," and ask the one question that makes it useful: "What's one thing I can do differently next time?" Read both the original thought and your response out loud. The out-loud part matters. It makes the replacement concrete and embodied rather than just intellectual. Do this with one self-critical thought today. Just one. You're not trying to overhaul your entire inner dialogue in a single sitting. You're practicing the replacement with one specific thought so you know what it feels like.

Action step two: Build the three-step self-compassion sequence into your response to setbacks over the next two weeks. The sequence is: name what happened in plain factual language, offer one sentence of honest acknowledgment that includes both the difficulty and the basic decency of your response to it, and ask what one thing you can take from this that helps you do it differently. Write the answers down each time. Don't do this from memory. The writing is part of the practice, because it forces specificity and prevents the sequence from collapsing back into vague self-reassurance. Every time you drift from your values, miss a commitment, or act in a way you're not proud of over the next two weeks, run this sequence within twenty-four hours. The speed of the response matters. The longer you wait, the more the self-critical story has time to solidify.

Action step three: Once each day for the next seven days, use the phrase "this is part of it" in a moment of genuine difficulty. Not as a dismissal of the difficulty. As a placement of it in context. Say it to yourself when the frustration rises, when the old pattern shows up again, when the week feels harder than it should, when you're tired of the work not being easier by now. "This is part of it." Write down the situation each time you use it and one sentence about what it felt like to say it rather than the alternative. After seven days, read back through what you wrote. Notice whether the phrase changed anything about how the difficult moments felt, even slightly. That change, however small, is the beginning of common humanity becoming a lived experience rather than just a concept you understand.

Action step four: Write one letter to yourself from the perspective of a genuinely supportive observer who knows your full history and still believes in your capacity to grow. This isn't a gratitude exercise or a list of your strengths. It's a letter that acknowledges specifically what you've been struggling with, places it in honest context, and speaks to your capacity for the return. Write it in second person, as if someone who knows you deeply and cares about you genuinely is writing to you. Give yourself at least fifteen minutes with this. Don't rush it. When you're done, read it out loud. Then keep it somewhere you can return to it when the inner critic is loudest. You're not creating a piece of false reassurance. You're creating an accurate, compassionate account of where you actually are, written from the perspective that self-criticism systematically prevents you from accessing on your own. That perspective is real. It just needs to be practiced until it becomes more available than the critical one.

The inner voice you carry through your growth matters as much as the tools you use for it. A harsh inner voice turns every setback into a reason to stop. A compassionate one turns every setback into a reason to return. The return is always the move. And the quality of your inner voice is what determines how quickly and how consistently you can make it.

Chapter Eleven

Case Studies: Anxiety and Depression

The principles in this book aren't just concepts that work in theory. They work in real life, with real people, facing the kind of internal chaos that makes getting out of bed feel like a genuine achievement some mornings. Anxiety and depression are two of the most common reasons people find themselves stuck at the reactive or regulated level of functioning, cycling through the same patterns, doing everything they've been told to do, and still feeling like they're missing something fundamental.

This chapter puts the Transcendent Functioning Model into direct contact with those two experiences. Not as a clinical manual, but as a practical illustration of what TFM actually looks like when applied to the specific texture of generalized anxiety and depression. The two hypothetical cases presented here are composites, not real individuals, but they reflect patterns that are genuinely common among people doing this kind of work. If you see yourself in either of them, that's the point.

What you'll find in these pages isn't a promise that TFM eliminates anxiety or depression. That's not the claim, and any framework making that claim should be treated with skepticism. What you'll find instead is a clear picture of how a person's relationship to those experiences can transformation so completely that the experiences themselves stop being the deciding factor in how they live. That transformation is real. It's achievable. And it changes everything.

Navigating the Hum of Apprehension

Sarah is a hypothetical 31-year-old teacher who has been living with generalized anxiety disorder for most of her adult life. She's smart, self-aware, and genuinely committed to her own growth. She's also exhausted. The worry doesn't take breaks. It moves from topic to topic with remarkable efficiency. Her career. Her relationships. Her health. Whether she said the right thing in a conversation three days ago. Whether she's making the right choices. Whether the unease she feels right now means something is about to go wrong.

She describes it as a hum. Not always loud, but always there. A low-level vibration of apprehension that colors everything.

Before working with TFM, Sarah's entire strategy was built around quieting the hum. She tried to think her way out of worries by analyzing them until they felt resolved. She avoided situations that might spike her anxiety, turning down social invitations when she was already feeling stretched, stepping back from professional opportunities that felt too exposed. She had a collection of calming techniques she rotated through. Some of them helped. None of them touched the underlying pattern.

She was regulated, but she wasn't free. And the regulated functioning was costing her more than she realized.

The first thing TFM offered Sarah wasn't a new calming technique. It was a different question entirely. Instead of "how do I make this anxiety stop?" the question became "what is this anxiety keeping me from that actually matters to me?" That question landed differently. It pointed somewhere she hadn't been looking.

When Sarah actually sat with that question, what emerged was a clear and specific answer.

Connection. She valued genuine closeness with other people more than almost anything else. But she'd been organizing her social life around protecting herself from the anxiety that social situations could trigger. She'd been managing the symptom so effectively that she'd quietly sacrificed the thing the symptom was keeping her from. Her world had gotten smaller, and she'd been calling that progress.

The cognitive defusion work came first, and for Sarah, it was genuinely difficult in the beginning. Her anxious thoughts didn't feel like thoughts. They felt like accurate threat assessments. "Something is going to go wrong at the dinner tonight" wasn't a mental event she was having. It was a reliable forecast. Getting distance from that certainty required repeated, specific practice with the labeling technique. "I'm having the thought that something will go wrong tonight." Said slowly. Said honestly. Not as a trick to dismiss the thought, but as a genuine act of observation.

What she noticed over the first two weeks of consistent practice was subtle but real. The thought still arrived. The physical anxiety response still fired. But there was a tiny gap that hadn't been there before. A moment where she could observe the thought rather than immediately inhabit it. That gap was small. It was also everything.

The defusion work alone wasn't enough, though. Sarah's anxiety had a physical dimension that thoughts couldn't reach. The tight chest before a social event. The restlessness that made sitting still feel impossible when worry was high. The shallow breathing she didn't even notice until someone pointed it out. This is where experiential expansion became central to her work.

She started practicing the body scan from Chapter 3, specifically during the moments when anxiety was already present rather than only in calm, controlled conditions. This was harder and more important than doing it preventively. When her chest was tight before a dinner she'd committed to attending, instead of running a calming technique to bring the sensation down, she turned toward it. She located it precisely. She described its qualities in her head. Tight. Warm. About the size of a fist, sitting just below her sternum. She watched it without trying to change it.

The first few times she did this, the sensation intensified briefly before it began to drop. That brief intensification was alarming. Her instinct was to pull back, to return to a calming strategy that would make it stop faster. She stayed with it instead. And what she discovered, through direct experience rather than theory, was that the sensation peaked and then began to subside on its own when she stopped fighting it. Not quickly. Not completely. But enough. Enough to demonstrate that the anxiety wasn't going to overwhelm her if she let herself feel it fully.

That discovery changed something at a deeper level than any technique had previously reached. The anxiety was no longer quite as threatening. Not because it was smaller, but because she'd proven to herself that she could hold it without being destroyed by it. The window of tolerance had widened slightly. And a wider window meant more room to choose her behavior rather than just react to the feeling.

The values work was where things became genuinely transformative for Sarah. She identified connection as her core value in the social domain. Genuine, honest, present-with-another-person connection. That value had been there her whole life. She'd just been letting anxiety veto it consistently. The transformation TFM offered wasn't about eliminating the anxiety before she could pursue connection. It was about pursuing connection with the anxiety present, because the connection mattered more than the comfort of avoiding the anxiety.

This required a specific kind of practice around uncertainty. Generalized anxiety disorder has a particularly close relationship with uncertainty intolerance. The worry machine runs on "what if," and the relief strategy is usually some version of seeking certainty or avoiding the uncertain situation entirely. Sarah had been doing both for years. She over-prepared for things she couldn't fully control. She avoided situations where the outcome was genuinely unknown. She replayed conversations afterward to try to establish that they'd gone well enough.

The TFM approach to uncertainty wasn't to eliminate it or to convince herself that things would be fine. It was to treat uncertainty as a normal feature of a life that's actually being lived. Not a problem to be solved before she could engage. A condition she could learn to be present with.

A specific practice that helped her here was

what might be called the uncertainty acknowledgment. When a "what if" thought arrived, instead of analyzing it toward resolution or dismissing it, she would say: "I don't know how this will go, and I'm going to [specific value-driven action] anyway." Not "it'll probably be fine." Not "stop worrying." Just the honest acknowledgment of uncertainty paired with the commitment to act from her values regardless. "I don't know if this dinner will feel awkward, and I'm going to go because I value the friendship." Said clearly. Said before the anxiety had a chance to build a full case for avoidance.

Over several months of this practice, Sarah's life changed in ways that symptom management had never produced. She started attending more social events. Not because the anxiety disappeared before she went, but because she stopped requiring it to disappear before she'd go. She initiated conversations she would previously have avoided. She took on a leadership role at her school that she'd been turning down for two years because the visibility felt too exposed. The anxiety was still present in many of these situations. It just wasn't running the show anymore.

The hum didn't go silent. But it stopped being

the loudest thing in the room.

There are three specific practices that emerged from Sarah's work that are directly applicable if anxiety is a central challenge for you. The first is what might be called the "values override" practice. When anxiety is pushing you toward avoidance, write down the specific thing you're considering avoiding and the specific value that the avoided action would express. Then write one sentence that names the anxiety honestly and commits to the action anyway: "I'm feeling anxious about [specific situation], and I'm choosing to [specific action] because I value [specific value]." Write it before you act. The writing makes the choice conscious rather than automatic. Do this every time you notice anxiety driving an avoidance decision over the next two weeks. Keep a record. After two weeks, count how many times you chose the value-driven action. That number is your evidence that you can act in the presence of anxiety rather than waiting for it to clear.

The second practice is the uncertainty acknowledgment, exactly as described above. When a "what if" thought arrives, respond with: "I don't know how this will go, and I'm going to [specific action] anyway." Say it out loud when you can. Write it down when you can't. Use it every time a "what if" thought is pushing you toward avoidance or over-preparation. The goal isn't to feel comfortable with uncertainty. The goal is to act from your values while uncertainty is present. Those are different things, and the second one is achievable right now.

The third practice is the body scan specifically during anxiety, not only during calm moments. The next time you notice anxiety rising before something you've committed to doing, pause for three minutes and run the body scan from Chapter 3. Locate the sensation. Describe its physical qualities. Watch it without trying to change it. Then do the thing you were going to do, with the sensation still present. This practice, repeated consistently, builds direct experiential evidence that you can feel anxiety at full intensity and still choose your behavior. That evidence is more powerful than any amount of reassurance, because it comes from your own lived experience rather than from someone telling you it'll be okay.

What Sarah's case illustrates most clearly is this: anxiety doesn't have to be absent for a full life to be possible. The goal was never to eliminate the hum. The goal was to stop letting the hum make all the decisions.

Reconnecting Through the Darkness

David is a hypothetical 42-year-old software engineer who describes his depression not as sadness, exactly, but as a kind of absence. The things that used to matter don't seem to matter the same way. The work he found genuinely engaging feels mechanical. The relationships he valued feel like obligations. The hobbies he used to pursue with real enthusiasm sit untouched. He's not in acute crisis. He's functioning. He goes to work. He meets his responsibilities. But there's a flatness to everything that makes the functioning feel hollow.

He describes it as living behind glass. Everything is visible. Nothing quite reaches him.

Depression creates a specific kind of trap that's different from anxiety's trap. Anxiety pushes you into avoidance through fear. Depression pulls you into inertia through the removal of the felt sense that anything matters enough to act on. The motivation that would normally carry you toward the things you value goes quiet. And without that motivational signal, the default is stillness. Waiting for the feeling to return. Waiting to want things again. Waiting to feel like yourself.

The waiting is the trap. Because the feeling rarely returns through waiting. It returns through action, and action is precisely what depression makes most difficult.

TFM offered David a way out of the waiting that didn't require him to feel motivated first. The central insight, which took him several weeks to actually believe through experience rather than just understand intellectually, was this: he didn't need to feel like doing the things that mattered to him in order to do them. The feeling could come after. Or not come at all. The action had value regardless.

The first challenge was identifying what he actually valued, because depression has a particular way of obscuring values. It doesn't just remove motivation. It can make the values themselves feel inaccessible, as if the things that once mattered were a different person's concerns. When David was asked what he valued, his first honest answer was "I don't know anymore." That answer was important. It wasn't a permanent truth. It was a symptom of the depression itself, the flatness extending into his sense of meaning.

The values clarification work for David required going further back than his current experience. He was asked to think about times before the depression deepened when he felt most like himself. Not necessarily happy, but genuinely present and engaged. What was he doing in those moments? Who was he with? What was he working on? This wasn't nostalgia for its own sake. It was archaeological work, digging beneath the layer of flatness to find what was still there underneath it.

What emerged was specific. He had valued craftsmanship, the particular satisfaction of building something well, whether that was code, a piece of furniture he'd worked on years ago, or a meal he'd taken real care with. He had valued mentoring, the experience of helping someone younger understand something difficult. He had valued humor, not performance humor but the genuine delight of finding something absurd together with another person. These weren't grand values. They were specific, textured, and real. And crucially, they were still his, even if he couldn't currently feel them.

The defusion work for David looked different

than it had for Sarah. His most damaging thoughts weren't "what if" spirals. They were quieter and more total. "Nothing I do makes much difference." "I used to care about this, which means the version of me that cared was probably just naive." "Getting started is pointless because I won't sustain it anyway." These thoughts weren't loud. They arrived with the quiet authority of obvious truths. And because they were quiet, they were harder to notice and harder to defuse from than the dramatic catastrophizing that anxiety often produces.

The labeling practice was particularly important here. "I'm having the thought that nothing I do makes much difference." Said slowly. Written down. Repeated enough times that the thought began to reveal itself as a thought rather than a fact. The depression wanted to present these thoughts as realistic assessments. The defusion practice kept returning to the same simple observation: this is a mental event. It's something my mind is producing right now. It may or may not be accurate. And it doesn't have to determine what I do next.

The experiential expansion component for David focused on something specific to depression: the experience of numbness itself. Depression often produces a paradoxical emotional experience where the person isn't feeling intense negative emotion so much as feeling very little. The numbness can be its own kind of suffering, the grief of not being able to grieve, the frustration of not being able to feel frustrated. Traditional expansion work focuses on allowing difficult emotions to be present without fighting them. For David, the work involved allowing the numbness to be present without fighting it either, without demanding that it transform into something more recognizable as feeling.

This was subtle and important. The impulse to force feeling, to watch a film that should be moving and feel nothing and then interpret the nothing as evidence of how far gone he was, was itself a form of struggle that amplified the suffering. The expansion practice asked him to let the numbness be what it was. To observe it without making it mean something catastrophic about his capacity for recovery. Numbness is a state. States change. The observation of a state, without the secondary layer of panic about the state, is what allows it to move.

The value-driven action work was where the most concrete and observable change happened for David. The key principle here was small and specific. Not grand re-engagement with life. Not a dramatic return to full vitality. One small action, connected to one genuine value, done regardless of whether he felt like doing it.

He started with craftsmanship. He committed to spending twenty minutes each evening working on a small woodworking project he'd abandoned eight months earlier. Not because he felt excited about it. Not because he expected it to feel meaningful. Because craftsmanship was something he had genuinely valued, and twenty minutes was achievable even on the flattest days. He used the two-minute rule from Chapter 5 to get started on the nights when even twenty minutes felt like too much. Two minutes of picking up the tools. That was the only commitment. The two minutes usually became more.

The first two weeks produced almost no felt sense of satisfaction. He did the twenty minutes. He put the tools down. The flatness remained. He kept going anyway, because the TFM framework had given him something important: the understanding that the absence of felt reward didn't mean the action was pointless. The value was being expressed through the doing, regardless of whether the doing felt good.

That was enough to keep going. By the third week, something small transformationed. Not a dramatic return of enthusiasm. A moment of genuine absorption. Ten minutes where the problem of fitting two pieces of wood together occupied his full attention and the flatness receded slightly. He noticed it. He didn't chase it or try to make it last. He just noted it as evidence that something was still there underneath the depression. The capacity for absorption hadn't been destroyed. It had been dormant.

The mentoring value was harder to act on because it required other people, and depression had made social engagement feel particularly costly. He started small here too. He agreed to answer one technical question per week from a junior colleague who had been asking for his input. One question. Written response. No face-to-face required. The commitment was so small it felt almost trivial. But it was connected to something real. He had valued the experience of helping someone understand a difficult thing. That value didn't require him to feel warm and engaged before he could express it. It just required him to write a thoughtful answer to one question.

The playful exploration element was perhaps the most counterintuitive part of David's work with TFM. Depression tends to produce a very serious, effortful relationship with recovery. Every action feels like it should be meaningful and productive. The idea of doing something with a spirit of lightness or curiosity rather than deliberate therapeutic intent felt almost frivolous. But it was important precisely because depression had stripped the playfulness from his engagement with the world, and reclaiming it, even in small ways, was part of reclaiming the texture of his own life.

He was encouraged to try one thing each week that he approached with genuine curiosity rather than a specific goal. Not to produce anything. Not to improve anything. Just to see what happened. He started cooking recipes he'd never tried before, not to become a better cook but because the combination of sensory engagement, problem-solving, and the absence of any real stakes made it a low-pressure way to be present in his own kitchen. Some of the recipes were terrible. He found that mildly funny. The mildly funny was something. It was more than the flatness had been offering.

Over several months, David's experience transformationed in ways that were gradual and real. The depression didn't lift dramatically. The flatness still came. But his relationship to it changed. He stopped waiting for it to clear before he would act. He stopped treating the absence of motivation as evidence that action was pointless. He developed what might be called a working relationship with his own low states, the ability to acknowledge them honestly while continuing to express his values through small, specific actions that didn't require him to feel well first.

The inertia, which had been the defining feature of his stuck state, began to loosen. Not because the depression disappeared, but because he'd stopped requiring it to disappear before he would move. The movement itself, value-driven and consistent, began to create small but real changes in his daily experience. Not euphoria. Not a return to some idealized previous version of himself. A more textured, more engaged, more genuinely his life than the one he'd been passively inhabiting.

Three specific practices emerge from David's case that are directly applicable if depression or low motivation is a central challenge for you. The first is the dormant values excavation. If your current depressed state makes your values feel inaccessible, go further back in your own history. Think about times when you felt most genuinely yourself, not necessarily happy, but present and engaged. Write down what you were doing. Look for patterns. What was there in those moments that isn't present now? Write two or three specific values that those moments point toward. These are still yours. The depression has obscured them. They haven't been destroyed.

The second practice is the smallest possible value-driven action, done daily regardless of felt motivation. Take one of the values you identified and commit to one action that expresses it, small enough to be achievable on your worst day. Not the action you'd take if you felt well. The action you can take as you actually are right now. Use the two-minute rule to start on the days when even small feels impossible. Do it every day for two weeks. Don't evaluate it based on how it feels while you're doing it. Evaluate it based on whether you did it. The doing is the point. The feeling may follow. It may not. The doing has value either way.

The third practice is the playful exploration

commitment. Once each week, do one thing with genuine curiosity and no specific goal. Something where the outcome genuinely doesn't matter. Cook something new. Rearrange something. Walk a route you've never taken. Try to fix something you don't know how to fix. Approach it with the spirit of "I wonder what happens" rather than "this needs to produce something." Depression creates a very earnest, effortful relationship with recovery. Playful exploration interrupts that pattern and begins to restore the lighter quality of engagement that makes a life feel like yours rather than just a set of managed obligations.

What David's case illustrates most clearly is that transcendent functioning in the context of depression isn't about manufacturing positive emotion or forcing yourself to feel engaged before you actually are. It's about acting from your values in the presence of the flatness, the numbness, the absence of motivation, treating those states as weather you can navigate rather than walls you have to dismantle before you can move. The movement is what gradually changes the weather. Not the other way around.

Recap and Action Steps

These two cases cover different terrain, but they share a common structure. In both, the person had been organized around their internal experience in a way that kept them stuck. Sarah was organized around managing and avoiding anxiety. David was organized around waiting for depression to lift before he would fully engage. Both were at the regulated level at best, and both were paying a significant price for it in the quality of their actual lives.

TFM didn't offer either of them a cure for their internal experience. It offered them a different relationship to it. One where the internal experience, however difficult, stopped having veto power over their choices. That transformation, from being managed by the internal state to acting from values in its presence, is the practical definition of transcendent functioning applied to real clinical challenges.

The principles that made the difference in both cases are worth stating plainly. Defusion allowed them to see their most damaging thoughts as mental events rather than facts. Experiential expansion allowed them to hold their most difficult internal experiences without immediately fleeing them. Values clarification gave them something to move toward that didn't depend on feeling well first. And committed action, small and specific and consistent, created the lived evidence that they were capable of expressing their values regardless of what their internal weather was doing.

None of this happened quickly. Neither case involved a dramatic turning point. Both involved weeks of practice that produced small, incremental transformations that accumulated over time into something genuinely different. That's how this works. Not in sudden transformations, but in the slow accumulation of small, consistent choices that gradually change the relationship between you and your own internal experience.

The action steps below are built directly from both cases. They're designed to be applicable whether anxiety, depression, or both are part of your experience. Work through them in the order given over the next three weeks.

Action step one: Identify which pattern is most

active for you right now. Read back through both cases and notice which one you recognized yourself in more strongly. You don't have to fit neatly into one category. But identifying whether your primary challenge is anxiety-driven avoidance or depression-driven inertia helps you choose the right starting point. Write one sentence that describes your current pattern as specifically as possible: "My primary stuck pattern right now is [specific description]." That sentence is your starting point for the work below.

Action step two: Identify one value that your current stuck pattern is most directly blocking. For anxiety, ask: what am I consistently avoiding that I actually care about? For depression, ask: what used to matter to me that I've stopped acting on? Write the value as a specific behavioral phrase, not a noun. Not "connection" but "I show up genuinely for the people I care about." Not "creativity" but "I make things with real care and attention." Write it down. Post it somewhere visible. This is the value your committed action will be built from.

Action step three: Design one small value-driven action for each of the next fourteen days. Small enough to be achievable on your worst day. Specific enough that you know exactly when you've done it. Connected clearly to the value you identified in step two. Write all fourteen actions in advance so you're not deciding each day whether to act and what to do. The decision has already been made. The only question each day is whether you do the thing you already committed to. Use the two-minute rule on the days when even the small action feels too heavy. Start with two minutes. See what happens.

Action step four: Run the defusion labeling practice specifically on your most disruptive thought pattern. If anxiety is your primary challenge, your most disruptive thought pattern is probably some version of "what if [feared outcome]." If depression is your primary challenge, it's probably some version of "nothing I do matters" or "I won't be able to sustain this." Write the specific thought down. Practice saying "I'm having the thought that..." followed by the thought, out loud, every morning for two weeks. This takes thirty seconds. Do it before you check your phone. The consistency is what builds the defusion capacity. Occasional practice produces occasional results. Daily practice produces a genuine transformation in your default relationship to the thought.

Action step five: Keep a two-week record of value-driven actions taken in the presence of difficult internal states. Each day, write one sentence about one action you took that was aligned with your values while anxiety, depression, numbness, or low motivation was also present. Not actions you took when you felt good. Actions you took while the difficult internal state was there. "I went to the dinner even though the anxiety was high." "I worked on the project for twenty minutes even though nothing felt meaningful." These entries are your evidence base. They're the record of your own demonstrated capacity to act from your values regardless of your emotional weather. After two weeks, read back through all fourteen entries. What you'll find there is more convincing than anything this book can tell you, because it's proof drawn from your own life, your own choices, your own demonstrated ability to operate above your internal state when you choose to. That proof is what makes the transformation from knowing these principles to actually living them something real and lasting rather than just temporarily motivating.

Chapter Twelve

Case Studies: Trauma and OCD

Some internal experiences don't just make life harder. They reorganize it entirely. Trauma and OCD occupy a different category than the anxiety and depression explored in the previous chapter. They reach deeper into the nervous system, deeper into the sense of self, and they tend to produce a relationship with internal experience that's more entrenched, more defended, and more resistant to the standard toolkit of self-improvement advice. If you've dealt with either of these, you already know that telling yourself to "just feel the feeling" can land as either useless or genuinely frightening, depending on the day.

That's why this chapter exists.

The two hypothetical cases here are composites that reflect patterns genuinely common among people working through trauma responses and OCD. They're not presented as clinical protocols or as promises about what treatment looks like in a professional setting. They're illustrations of how TFM's core processes, defusion, experiential expansion, attachment reduction, and value-driven action, apply when the internal landscape is more complex and the stakes of getting it wrong feel higher. What you'll find in both cases is the same fundamental transformation that has run through every chapter of this book: from being organized around controlling internal experience to being guided by values in its presence. That transformation doesn't become less relevant when the internal experience is more severe. If anything, it becomes more important.

The principles don't change. The pacing and the gentleness with which they're applied do.

Healing the Fractured Self

Maria is a hypothetical woman in her late twenties who sought support following a period of significant psychological distress connected to a traumatic experience several years earlier. The details of what happened were difficult for her to articulate, even in a space where she felt relatively safe. What she could describe was the aftermath. A constant low-level vigilance that never fully switched off. Intrusive images and memories that arrived without warning and felt, in those moments, like they were happening again rather than being remembered. A deep, persistent sense that she was somehow broken in a way that couldn't be repaired. And a lifestyle built almost entirely around avoiding anything that might trigger the memories to surface.

She had stopped going to certain parts of her city. She avoided specific songs, certain smells, particular kinds of conversations. She turned down invitations that might put her in situations she couldn't fully control. She described her world as having gotten very small, and she described herself as having gotten very tired of living in it.

Her stated goal when she began working with TFM principles was clear and understandable: she wanted the memories gone. She wanted to feel normal again. She wanted the past to stop reaching into the present and taking things from her. That goal made complete sense. And it was also, in the form she was holding it, a significant part of what was keeping her stuck.

The first thing TFM offered Maria wasn't a technique. It was a reframe of what safety actually means. She had been operating from the assumption that safety was the absence of discomfort. That she would feel safe when the memories stopped coming, when the anxiety dropped, when the vigilance finally switched off. TFM proposed something different: that safety is the presence of your capacity to cope, not the absence of discomfort. That distinction sounds small. For Maria, it was the beginning of everything.

If safety requires the absence of difficult internal experience, then every intrusive memory is a threat to safety. Every anxiety spike is evidence of danger. Every moment of distress confirms that something is still wrong, still unresolved, still capable of destroying her. The entire internal world becomes a minefield. And the only response to a minefield is to stop moving.

If safety is the presence of coping capacity, the equation changes entirely. The intrusive memory arrives. It's painful. And she can hold it. She doesn't have to be destroyed by it. Her capacity to cope with it, built through practice, is what makes her safe. Not the absence of the memory. Her relationship to it.

This reframe didn't land immediately. It took weeks of returning to it before it started to feel like something more than a clever idea. The work that made it real was the work of gentle exposure, which is different from the kind of exposure work that asks someone to confront the most distressing material head-on from the start.

Gentle exposure begins at the edges. Not with the core traumatic memory but with the peripheral triggers, the things that are connected to it but carry less charge. For Maria, this meant starting with something as simple as walking through a neighborhood she'd been avoiding because it was adjacent to, but not directly connected to, the original trauma. The anxiety that arose was real. She located it in her body using the somatic awareness practice from Chapter 3. She described its qualities. She watched it without fighting it. And she walked through the neighborhood.

The first time, she felt shaky afterward. The second time, slightly less so. By the fifth time, the anxiety was present but no longer overwhelming. She had built direct evidence, through her own body and her own choices, that she could be in that neighborhood and survive it. That evidence was more powerful than any reassurance anyone could have offered her, because it came from her own experience rather than someone else's words.

The defusion work was particularly important for Maria because trauma has a specific relationship with cognitive fusion that's worth understanding clearly. Traumatic memories don't usually arrive as neutral recollections. They arrive with the full emotional and physical weight of the original experience. When an intrusive image surfaced for Maria, she didn't experience it as a memory. She experienced it as present-tense reality. The fusion between the memory and the current moment was nearly total. The past was happening now.

The labeling practice had to be applied gently and specifically. Not "I'm having the thought that I'm in danger" but something more precise: "I'm having a memory. This is the past arriving in the present. I'm here now, not there then." That distinction, between memory and current reality, is the specific defusion work that trauma requires. It doesn't deny the memory. It doesn't minimize what happened. It places the memory in its correct temporal location. The past is the past. Right now, in this moment, she is here. And here is safe enough to stay in.

She practiced this every time an intrusive image or memory arrived. Not by pushing the memory away. By observing it, labeling it as a memory, and then deliberately orienting her attention to something in her present physical environment. The feel of her feet on the floor. The sound of something in the room. The temperature of the air on her skin. These weren't distractions. They were anchors. They were ways of confirming, through sensory experience, that the present moment was real and distinct from the past one that the memory was pulling her toward.

The experiential expansion component for Maria required a particular kind of pacing that's worth describing in detail. Standard expansion practice asks you to turn toward difficult internal experience and allow it to be present. For someone with trauma, that instruction needs to be graduated carefully. Turning toward a traumatic memory at full intensity, without preparation, without the right conditions, without adequate coping capacity already established, can be retraumatizing rather than healing. The gentleness isn't optional. It's the whole point.

Maria worked with the edges of her experience before the center. She practiced allowing small amounts of anxiety to be present without immediately escaping them. She practiced staying with mild discomfort, the kind produced by the peripheral triggers, until she had direct evidence that she could hold it. She built her window of tolerance gradually, from the outside in, rather than trying to jump immediately to the core material.

What she discovered through this gradual process was something that surprised her. The sensations associated with her traumatic memories, when approached slowly and with genuine curiosity rather than terror, had more texture and more variability than she had expected. They weren't a monolithic wall of overwhelming feeling. They were specific sensations that transformationed, moved, changed in intensity, and, crucially, sometimes dropped on their own when she stopped fighting them. That discovery, made through direct experience over many weeks, changed her relationship to the memories themselves. They were still painful. They were no longer quite as totalizing.

The attachment reduction work for Maria centered on one specific and deeply held attachment: the belief that she needed to be the person she was before the trauma in order to be okay. She had been grieving a version of herself that she felt the trauma had taken. The person who moved through the world without hypervigilance. The person who didn't have to plan every social situation around potential triggers. The person who felt, in her own words, "normal." She was attached to that version of herself with a grief that was real and valid and also, at the same time, keeping her from inhabiting the person she actually was now.

The TFM approach to this wasn't to tell her that the grief was wrong or that she should simply accept what happened and move on. The grief was legitimate. The attachment was understandable. The question was whether the attachment was serving her. Whether holding tightly to the "before" version of herself was helping her build a life now, or whether it was keeping her in a permanent state of mourning for something she couldn't get back.

She was invited to consider a different framing. Not that the trauma was okay or that it hadn't cost her something real. But that the person she was now, the person who had survived something genuinely difficult and was still here, still trying, still capable of caring about her own life, that person had value and capacity that the "before" version hadn't yet had to develop. Resilience isn't built in the absence of difficulty. It's built through it. She wasn't less than who she was before. She was different. And different could still be enough.

This reframe didn't dissolve the grief. But it created a small amount of room alongside the grief for something else. A beginning acknowledgment that who she was now was worth investing in, even if it wasn't who she'd planned to be.

The values work came as the other pieces began to establish themselves. Maria had spent so long organizing her life around avoidance that identifying what she actually wanted to move toward required genuine excavation. When she finally got beneath the "I want to feel normal" answer, what she found was specific and textured. She valued creative work. She had been a visual artist before the trauma and had stopped completely. She valued honest friendship, the kind where you could say something real and be received rather than managed. She valued being present in her own life rather than always slightly elsewhere, always slightly braced for the next intrusion.

These values became the compass that guided

her gentle exposure work. She wasn't exposing herself to triggers for the sake of exposure. She was moving toward things that mattered to her, and the triggers happened to be in the way. The distinction changed the quality of the work entirely. She wasn't doing something difficult because a framework told her to. She was doing something difficult because connection and creativity and presence mattered to her, and those things were on the other side of the discomfort she'd been avoiding.

She started painting again. Small pieces at first, in a corner of her apartment, for twenty minutes at a time. The creative work didn't feel joyful immediately. It felt effortful and strange, like relearning a language she'd once been fluent in. But it was hers. And doing it, even badly, even with the hypervigilance still humming in the background, was an act of reclaiming something the trauma had taken from her. Not by eliminating the trauma's effects. By refusing to let those effects be the only thing that defined her daily life.

Over months of this work, Maria's life expanded. Not dramatically. Not in a straight line. There were weeks where the intrusive memories were louder, where the avoidance pulled harder, where the grief about what the trauma had cost her felt fresh and sharp. But the expansion was real and cumulative. She was going more places. Saying yes to more things. Creating work that felt genuinely hers. The memories still came. They had less authority over her choices than they used to.

There are three specific practices from Maria's case that are directly applicable if trauma responses are part of your experience. Before engaging with any of them, one thing is worth saying clearly: if you're working with significant trauma, doing so with professional support alongside these practices is genuinely important. TFM principles are compatible with professional trauma treatment. They're not a replacement for it.

The first practice is the temporal anchoring technique for intrusive memories. When a traumatic memory arrives, say to yourself: "This is a memory. This happened then. I am here now." Then orient your attention to three specific sensory details of your current physical environment. Name them out loud if you can. The floor beneath your feet. A sound in the room. The temperature of the air. You're not dismissing the memory. You're placing it correctly in time and anchoring yourself in the present moment.

Practice this every time an intrusive memory arrives over the next two weeks. Write down each instance and one sentence about what you noticed. The record builds evidence that the technique works, which makes it more available in the moments when you need it most.

The second practice is peripheral gentle exposure. Identify one thing you've been avoiding that sits at the edges of your trauma response, not the core trigger but something connected to it, something that produces anxiety but not overwhelming distress. Commit to one brief, specific contact with that thing this week. Walk past the place. Listen to the song for thirty seconds. Have a short version of the conversation. Use the body scan to observe what arises without fighting it. Then leave. That's the complete practice. One brief, boundaried contact. Write down what happened in your body and what you noticed about the anxiety's trajectory. Did it peak and begin to drop? Did it stay constant? Did it transformation? That information tells you about your current window of tolerance and how it's developing.

The third practice is the safety reframe, applied daily. Each morning, write one sentence that completes this phrase: "My safety today comes from my capacity to..." and fill in something specific. "My capacity to notice when I'm overwhelmed and step back." "My capacity to stay with discomfort for a few minutes before it peaks." "My capacity to return to my values even after a difficult day." You're not performing positivity. You're deliberately building a different definition of safety, one that's located in your own demonstrated capacities rather than in the absence of difficulty. Over time, that definition becomes more real and more available than the old one.

Breaking the Prison of Ritual

John is a hypothetical man in his mid-thirties who has been living with OCD for over a decade. His particular presentation involves contamination obsessions and checking compulsions, but the structure of his experience is one that people with many different OCD presentations will recognize. The intrusive thought arrives. It's disturbing and it feels urgent. The anxiety spikes almost immediately. And then the compulsion offers itself as relief, a ritual, a checking behavior, a mental review, something that will neutralize the thought and bring the anxiety down. He does the compulsion. The anxiety drops. For a while.

Then the cycle begins again.

John described his life as a series of negotiations with his own mind. He knew, intellectually and clearly, that washing his hands for the tenth time wouldn't actually prevent harm. He knew the intrusive thoughts weren't reliable indicators of real danger. He knew the rituals were irrational. He knew all of this. And he did the rituals anyway, because the knowing didn't touch the feeling, and the feeling was the thing that was running his life.

"It's like being trapped in a prison of my own mind," he said. "I know the walls aren't real. But I can't get out."

OCD has a specific relationship with TFM that's worth understanding before getting into the practical work. The compulsive cycle is, at its core, an extreme version of experiential avoidance. The intrusive thought produces anxiety. The compulsion is the avoidance strategy. The anxiety drops temporarily. The avoidance is reinforced. The cycle tightens. What makes OCD particularly resistant to standard approaches is that the relief produced by compulsions is real and immediate, which means the reinforcement is powerful and consistent. The brain has learned, through thousands of repetitions, that the compulsion is the solution to the anxiety. Unlearning that equation takes time, consistency, and a specific kind of willingness to tolerate the anxiety without performing the compulsion.

TFM doesn't ask John to simply stop doing the compulsions. That instruction, without the supporting framework, tends to produce white-knuckle suppression that's unsustainable. What TFM offers instead is a gradual restructuring of his relationship to the thoughts and the anxiety, so that the compulsion becomes less necessary rather than just less performed.

The defusion work was the starting point, and it had to be applied with precision. OCD thoughts have a particular quality that makes them especially sticky. They feel morally significant. They feel like the kind of thoughts that a dangerous or defective person would have. The fusion isn't just "this thought is true." It's "the fact that I'm having this thought says something terrible about who I am." That second layer of fusion, the fusion with the self-meaning of the thought, is often what makes OCD thoughts feel so urgent and so impossible to simply observe.

The defusion practice for John began with the most basic form of labeling. When a contamination thought arrived, instead of immediately engaging with the checking ritual, he was guided to say: "I'm noticing a thought about contamination." Not "I might be contaminated." Not "what if I contaminated something?" Just: "I'm noticing a thought about contamination." The transformation from first-person identification with the thought to third-person observation of it was the target. He wasn't the thought. He was the person noticing the thought.

This was genuinely difficult in the beginning. The thoughts arrived with such urgency, such felt significance, that stepping back from them felt almost impossible. He described it as trying to observe a fire alarm from a calm distance while the alarm was actively blaring. The defusion practice didn't silence the alarm. It changed his relationship to the sound. The alarm was still going. But he was beginning to recognize it as an alarm rather than as proof of an actual fire.

A specific adaptation of the defusion work that helped John was naming the OCD as a distinct voice rather than as his own thinking. He started referring to the intrusive thoughts as "the OCD talking" rather than as his own thoughts. "The OCD is saying there's contamination risk." "The OCD is insisting I need to check." This externalization didn't mean he was denying that the thoughts were happening in his mind. It meant he was creating enough distance from them to recognize that they represented a specific, identifiable pattern rather than accurate information about reality. That distance was small but crucial.

The experiential expansion work for OCD is the component that most directly addresses the compulsive cycle, and it maps closely onto the urge surfing practice from Chapter 3. The core skill being built is the ability to feel the anxiety and the urge to perform the compulsion without acting on the urge. This is what's sometimes called tolerating the itch. Not scratching it. Sitting with the discomfort of the itch until it naturally subsides.

John started this practice with the lowest-anxiety items in his compulsive repertoire. Not the most distressing contamination scenarios but the mildest ones. He identified a situation where the urge to check was present but not overwhelming, something like touching a doorknob and then feeling the pull to wash his hands. He agreed to wait five minutes before washing. Not to never wash. Just to wait five minutes.

The five minutes were uncomfortable. He was asked to use the somatic awareness practice during that time. To locate the anxiety and the urge in his body. To describe their physical qualities. To watch them without acting on them. The first few times, the anxiety felt like it was building rather than dropping. He stayed with it anyway. And then, around the four-minute mark, something transformationed. The urge began to lose intensity. Not completely. Not permanently. But measurably. He could feel it dropping.

That experience was significant in a way that no amount of explanation could have produced. He had direct, bodily evidence that the urge didn't keep building forever. It peaked. It dropped. He didn't have to perform the compulsion to make it go away. It would go away on its own if he could tolerate the discomfort long enough to let it. The compulsion wasn't the only exit from the anxiety. Time and tolerance were also exits. And unlike the compulsion, they didn't reinforce the cycle.

He extended the waiting period gradually over

several weeks. Five minutes became ten. Ten became twenty. The compulsion was still available. He was choosing not to use it, not through suppression but through the practiced recognition that the urge would pass without it. Each successful wait built more evidence. Each piece of evidence made the next wait slightly more accessible. The cycle was beginning to loosen, not because the thoughts stopped coming but because his relationship to the urgency they produced was changing.

The attachment reduction work for John centered on two specific attachments that were driving the compulsive cycle. The first was his attachment to certainty. OCD has been described as a disorder of doubt, and the compulsions are, at their core, attempts to achieve certainty in a world that doesn't offer it. John was deeply attached to the idea that he could, through sufficient checking and ritual, achieve a state of confirmed safety. That state was never actually achieved, which is why the checking had to keep happening. The certainty always needed to be reconfirmed because certainty, in the form he was seeking it, isn't available.

The TFM approach to this attachment wasn't to

tell John that certainty doesn't exist, which he already knew intellectually. It was to help him practice tolerating uncertainty in small, specific, graduated doses. He started with the lowest-stakes uncertainties in his life, situations where the outcome genuinely didn't matter much but where he noticed the pull toward checking or confirming. He practiced leaving those uncertainties unresolved because tolerating it in small doses was building a capacity that he needed for the larger ones.

The second attachment was to the idea that a "good enough" life wasn't enough. OCD often produces a standard of purity or safety that's absolute. Anything less than complete certainty of safety is experienced as unacceptable. John had been living by a standard that required zero risk, zero contamination, zero possibility of harm. That standard was both impossible and exhausting. It meant that any ordinary daily activity that carried even minimal uncertainty triggered the compulsive cycle.

The TFM reframe here was the concept of a "good enough" life. Not a perfect life. Not a risk-free life. A life where reasonable precautions are taken, where real risks are addressed, and where the remaining uncertainty is accepted as the normal texture of being alive rather than as an intolerable threat. This wasn't about lowering standards. It was about calibrating them to what's actually achievable and what's actually necessary. A reasonable level of hygiene is achievable and necessary. Absolute certainty of zero contamination is neither.

John was guided to identify what "reasonable" looked like for specific situations. Washing hands after using the bathroom: reasonable. Washing hands after touching a doorknob in his own home: not necessary. Checking that the stove is off once before leaving: reasonable. Checking it seven times and then driving back to check again: the OCD's standard, not a reasonable one. These distinctions, made explicitly and repeatedly, helped him build a different reference point for his behavior. Not what the OCD required. What a thoughtful, reasonable person would actually do in this situation.

The values work for John was where the transformation from managing symptoms to building a life became most concrete. He identified three values that the OCD had been quietly dismantling for years. Presence, the ability to be fully engaged in what was happening around him rather than partly occupied with monitoring and ritual. Connection, genuine closeness with the people he cared about, which required the kind of relaxed, unguarded engagement that the OCD made nearly impossible. And contribution, the sense of being useful and effective in his work and in his relationships, which was hard to access when a significant portion of his mental bandwidth was consumed by the compulsive cycle.

These values gave him a reason to do the difficult work of tolerating the urges that went beyond symptom reduction. He wasn't just trying to have fewer compulsions. He was trying to reclaim presence, connection, and contribution. The compulsions were obstacles to those things. And those things mattered more to him than the temporary relief the compulsions provided.

A specific practice that emerged from this values work was what might be called the "OCD tax" awareness. Each time he performed a compulsion, he was asked to note briefly what it cost him in terms of his values. Not in a punishing way. As honest accounting. "That ritual took four minutes and left me feeling ashamed, which made me less present in the conversation with my partner immediately afterward." The OCD tax was real and specific. Seeing it clearly, rather than just experiencing it as vague exhaustion, gave him more concrete motivation to practice tolerating the urges. He wasn't just tolerating discomfort for the sake of it. He was trading a short-term reduction in anxiety for a longer-term investment in the life he actually wanted.

Progress for John was nonlinear, as it is for almost everyone working with OCD. There were weeks where the compulsive cycle loosened significantly and he felt genuinely freer. There were other weeks where stress or fatigue brought the OCD back with renewed force and the rituals increased. He learned to treat the difficult weeks not as evidence that the work wasn't working but as information about what conditions made his OCD more active. Stress, sleep deprivation, and periods of significant uncertainty were his main triggers. Knowing that didn't eliminate the difficult weeks. It made them less catastrophic, because he understood what was happening and knew what to do about it.

Over time, the prison John had described began to have more doors in it. The walls were still there. But he was moving through them more often, choosing his values over the compulsions more consistently, and building a life that, while not free from OCD's presence, was no longer entirely organized around its demands.

Three specific practices emerge from John's case that are applicable if OCD or compulsive patterns are part of your experience. As with the trauma section, a clear note: OCD responds well to professional treatment, specifically Exposure and Response Prevention therapy, and TFM principles work best alongside that kind of support rather than as a standalone replacement for it.

The first practice is the urge surfing sequence, applied to one low-anxiety compulsive situation this week. Identify the mildest compulsive urge in your current repertoire. When it arises, name it: "I'm noticing an urge to [specific behavior]." Locate it in your body. Describe its physical qualities. Set a timer for five minutes. Watch the urge without acting on it, using the somatic awareness practice to stay present with the physical experience. When the timer goes off, note what happened to the intensity. Did it peak? Did it drop? Write one sentence about what you observed. Do this with the same low-anxiety urge every day for one week. The evidence you're building is direct and specific:

the urge passes without the compulsion. That evidence, accumulated over seven days, begins to challenge the core OCD belief that the compulsion is necessary.

The second practice is the "OCD talking" defusion technique. Every time an intrusive OCD thought arrives, label it explicitly: "The OCD is saying [thought content]." Out loud when you can. Silently when you can't. Do this for two weeks, every time an OCD thought arrives. You're not arguing with the thought. You're not trying to prove it wrong. You're simply identifying its source. That identification, practiced consistently, begins to create the distance between you and the thought that makes the compulsion feel less mandatory.

The third practice is the "good enough" calibration for one specific OCD situation. Choose one situation where your OCD standard is clearly higher than what a reasonable person would require. Write down what the OCD demands. Then write down what a thoughtful, reasonable person would actually do in that situation. Commit to the reasonable standard for one week. Every time the OCD tries to pull you back to its standard, acknowledge the pull, label it as the OCD talking, and return to the reasonable standard. Write down each instance. After one week, review what happened. How many times did you hold the reasonable standard? What did the anxiety do when you did? That record is your evidence that the reasonable standard is survivable, which is the foundation for gradually extending it to more situations.

Recap and Action Steps

Both Maria and John were operating at the reactive and regulated levels for years before working with TFM principles. Maria's life had organized itself around avoiding trauma triggers. John's had organized itself around performing compulsions to neutralize intrusive thoughts. Both were doing enormous amounts of work to manage their internal experience. Neither was free.

The transformation TFM offered both of them wasn't a cure for what they were experiencing. It was a fundamental change in their relationship to it. Maria stopped requiring the memories to be gone before she could reclaim her life. John stopped requiring the anxiety to be neutralized before he could act from his values. Both of them began to discover what operating above their internal experience actually meant in the context of genuinely difficult psychological challenges: not the absence of the difficulty, but the refusal to let the difficulty be the last word on how they lived.

Several principles ran through both cases and are worth naming plainly. Safety is the presence of coping capacity, not the absence of discomfort. That principle was central for Maria and it applies to anyone whose avoidance is organized around the idea that they need to feel safe before they can engage. The coping capacity is built through engagement, not before it. The engagement is what creates the safety.

The urge doesn't require the compulsion. That principle was central for John and it applies to anyone whose avoidance takes the form of neutralizing behavior, whether that's OCD rituals, reassurance-seeking, perfectionism, or any other compulsive pattern. The urge peaks and drops on its own. Every time you discover this through direct experience, the compulsion loses a small amount of its authority. That authority, eroded consistently over time, is what the freedom on the other side of OCD is built from.

Gentle exposure is not optional for trauma or OCD work. The word "gentle" matters. This isn't about forcing yourself into overwhelming situations without adequate support or preparation. It's about moving toward the edges of what's difficult, in small and boundaried ways, consistently enough that the window of tolerance expands and the feared experience loses some of its totalizing power. The gentleness is what makes it sustainable. The consistency is what makes it effective.

Values are what make the difficult work worth doing. Both Maria and John needed a reason to tolerate the discomfort of changing their relationship to their internal experience that went beyond symptom reduction. Symptom reduction alone wasn't enough motivation to sustain the work through the difficult weeks. Values were. Connection, creativity, presence, contribution. These things mattered more than the temporary comfort of avoidance. Keeping that truth alive and specific, not as an abstract idea but as a concrete daily reference point, was what kept both of them moving when the work was hard.

The action steps below are designed to be worked through in sequence over the next three weeks. They draw from both cases and are applicable whether trauma, OCD, or a combination of compulsive and avoidant patterns is your primary challenge.

Action step one: Identify your primary safety behavior. A safety behavior is any action you take to reduce anxiety or avoid distress that, over time, narrows your life rather than expanding it. For trauma, this might be avoiding specific places, people, topics, or sensory triggers. For OCD, it's the compulsive rituals. For other patterns, it might be reassurance-seeking, over-preparation, or staying in situations that feel controlled. Write down your primary safety behavior with specific detail. Not "I avoid things that make me anxious" but "I avoid [specific situations] because they trigger [specific internal experience] and I respond by [specific behavior]." The specificity matters. Vague awareness of a pattern is much harder to work with than a clearly named one.

Action step two: Identify the value that your primary safety behavior is most directly blocking. What is the safety behavior keeping you from? What would be possible in your life if the safety behavior were less dominant? Write the value as a behavioral phrase. Not "I value freedom" but "I move through the world without organizing my choices around what might trigger me." Not "I value peace" but "I engage fully in my daily life without the compulsive cycle consuming my attention." That phrase is where you're heading. It's the direction your committed action will point toward.

Action step three: Design one gentle exposure practice for this week. Start at the edges of your avoidance, not the center. Identify one situation, one trigger, one urge that sits at the lower end of your anxiety hierarchy. Design a brief, boundaried contact with it. Specific duration. Specific context. Clear endpoint. Use the somatic awareness practice during the contact to observe without fighting. Write down what happened to the anxiety during and after. That record is your evidence base. It starts small and builds. One gentle exposure this week. Two next week. The pace is yours. The direction is consistent.

Action step four: Practice the reframe of safety once each morning for two weeks. Each morning, write one sentence that completes this: "My safety today comes from my capacity to..." Fill it in with something specific and real. Something you've actually demonstrated through your own behavior.

Not aspirational. Evidenced. "My capacity to stay with the anxiety for five minutes without acting on the compulsion." "My capacity to walk through the difficult neighborhood and come out the other side." "My capacity to notice the intrusive memory and orient back to the present moment." After two weeks, read back through all fourteen sentences. What you'll find is a record of your own demonstrated coping capacity. That record is what makes the reframe real rather than just hopeful. Safety built from evidence is more durable than safety built from reassurance.

Chapter Thirteen

Daily Integration: TFM as a Lifestyle

You've built something real across the previous twelve chapters. The defusion skills. The expanded tolerance for difficult feelings. The loosened grip on rigid outcomes and self-narratives. The capacity to act from your values even when the internal weather isn't cooperating. The self-compassion that makes returning to your values possible without the spiral of self-punishment. These aren't just ideas you've read. They're capacities you've been developing through specific, repeated practice.

The question this chapter addresses is the one that determines whether any of it actually sticks.

How do you live this? Not in a retreat setting, not in a quiet morning practice, not in the ideal conditions you can sometimes create when life cooperates. How do you live it on a Tuesday afternoon when your inbox is full, your focus is scattered, and the last thing you feel like doing is being psychologically flexible? How do you carry transcendent functioning into the grocery store, the commute, the difficult conversation you didn't plan for, the moment when everything you've been building gets tested by the ordinary chaos of an actual life?

That's what this chapter is about. Not new concepts. The integration of everything you already have into the texture of daily living.

Weaving Presence into the Mundane

Most people think of psychological practice as something that happens in dedicated time. The morning meditation. The journaling session. The therapy appointment. These structured moments matter. But they're not where most of your life happens. Most of your life happens in the gaps between them. The commute. The walk to the kitchen. The three minutes waiting for a meeting to start. The lunch you eat while scrolling. The transition between one task and the next. These moments feel unremarkable, which is exactly why they're so important.

They're where your default operating mode runs unchecked.

If your default between structured practices is reactive functioning, then the structured practices are doing constant repair work on a foundation that keeps eroding. But if you can bring even partial presence into the ordinary moments, those moments become the practice. And the practice becomes continuous rather than scheduled.

This doesn't require more time. It requires a different quality of attention applied to time you're already spending.

The morning routine is the most important place to start, not because morning is inherently special but because how you begin tends to shape how you continue. Most people's mornings are reactive from the first conscious moment. The phone gets checked before the feet hit the floor. The notifications set the agenda before you've had a chance to set it yourself. The day's anxieties arrive before you've had a moment to choose your orientation toward them. You're already in managed mode before breakfast.

A specific restructuring of the first ten minutes changes this significantly. Before you check your phone, before you open any app, before the external world gets its first claim on your attention, do three things in sequence. First, take three slow, deliberate breaths. Not as a calming technique. As an act of orientation. You're signaling to your nervous system that you're awake and choosing, not just reacting. Second, ask yourself one question out loud or in your head: "What do I value most today?" Not what you need to accomplish. What you value. The distinction matters because it sets your compass before the day's demands set it for you. Third, identify one specific action that expresses that value before noon. Write it down somewhere you'll see it. That's the complete practice. Three breaths, one values question, one specific action. It takes less than two minutes and it changes the quality of what follows.

Consider someone like Priya, a hypothetical 29-year-old product manager who starts her days in a state of low-level dread. Her mornings used to begin with immediate phone-checking, which meant she was already responding to other people's priorities before she'd formed any of her own. She'd arrive at her desk feeling like she was behind before she'd started. When she restructured her first ten minutes using the sequence above, something transformationed within a week. Not dramatically. The dread didn't disappear. But she noticed that she was arriving at her desk with a direction rather than just a list of demands. She'd already answered the question of what mattered most that day. Everything else got filtered through that answer rather than replacing it.

The commute is the second major opportunity that most people completely waste. Whether it's twenty minutes on public transport, a drive, or a walk between rooms in a home office, the transition between home and work is a natural threshold. Most people fill it with podcasts, music, social media, or the mental rehearsal of everything that could go wrong in the day ahead. None of these are wrong, exactly. But they're all forms of filling the space rather than using it.

A commute presence practice uses that time specifically. If you're walking or on public transport, try this: for five minutes of your commute, put the earbuds away. Direct your attention to three specific sensory details of your immediate environment. The temperature of the air. The quality of the light. The specific sounds around you. Not as a meditation exercise. As a deliberate act of being in the moment you're actually in rather than the one you're rehearsing or avoiding. You're practicing the present-moment contact that transcendent functioning runs on.

You're doing it in an ordinary moment, which is exactly where it needs to work.

If you drive, the sensory focus transformations to what's immediately in front of you. The feel of the wheel. The specific quality of the light on the road. The sounds inside and outside the car. Five minutes. No content input. Just presence in the actual moment you're moving through. This isn't about making the commute spiritual. It's about using a transition that's already happening to practice the attentional skill that everything else in this book depends on.

Work breaks are the third ordinary moment that most people handle in ways that actively undermine their capacity for presence. The standard break involves switching from one screen to another, trading the work problem for the social media feed, the news, or the group chat. The nervous system doesn't actually rest during this kind of break. It just changes its input. What it needs, what actually restores attentional capacity, is a brief period of genuine disengagement from information.

A two-minute sensory grounding practice during work breaks does this specifically. When you take a break, step away from your screen completely. Stand up. Direct your attention to your five senses in sequence. What do you see right now, specifically? What do you hear? What do you feel physically, the temperature, the surface beneath your feet, the weight of your body? What do you smell? What do you taste? Move through each sense deliberately, taking about twenty seconds per sense. The whole sequence takes less than two minutes. What it does is bring your attention fully into the present moment and out of the cognitive loop of work demands and anticipatory thinking. Your nervous system registers the break as an actual break rather than just a change of content. You return to work with more genuine capacity than you left with.

The deeper principle running through all three of these practices is the same. Ordinary moments are opportunities for defusion and sensory grounding when you treat them that way. The morning routine can be a moment of values-setting or a moment of reactive absorption into other people's priorities. The commute can be a moment of present-moment practice or a moment of anticipatory worry. The work break can be a moment of genuine restoration or a moment of continued information consumption dressed up as rest. The moment is the same either way. Your relationship to it is the variable. And your relationship to it, practiced consistently across hundreds of ordinary moments, is what builds the capacity for transcendent functioning as a genuine daily reality rather than a peak state you occasionally access.

One more practice worth building into your ordinary day is what might be called the defusion check-in. Three times each day, at consistent times you choose in advance, pause for thirty seconds and ask: "What thought is currently running in the background?" Not the thought you're consciously working on. The one that's running underneath it. The low-grade worry. The recurring self-critical loop. The anticipatory dread about something coming up. Name it. Label it as a thought: "I'm having the thought that..." Say it once. Then return to what you were doing. You're not trying to resolve the thought or work through it. You're practicing the observer stance in the middle of your actual day, in the moments when it's hardest to access and most necessary to have.

Set three alarms on your phone for these check-ins. Label them "defusion check." When they go off, do the thirty-second practice regardless of what you're doing. The consistency of the timing is what builds the habit. After two weeks of this, most people report that they start catching the background thought without needing the alarm. The metacognitive awareness that the practice was developing has become more automatic. That's the goal. Not the alarm. The awareness the alarm was training.

Intentional Structures and Routines

Presence in the moment is necessary. It's not sufficient on its own. What keeps you moving in a consistent direction over days, weeks, and months is structure. Not rigid structure that collapses when life disrupts it, but intentional structure that holds your direction even when your motivation fluctuates, your mood transformations, and the circumstances around you change in ways you didn't plan for. This section is about building that structure using three specific tools: journaling, value-lists, and end-of-day reflections. Together, they create a daily architecture that consolidates your growth and keeps your compass calibrated without requiring perfect conditions to function.

Journaling is one of the most frequently

recommended practices in the self-development space and one of the least effectively used. Most people either don't journal at all or only journal in ways that produce emotional processing without behavioral direction. *They write about how they feel. They don't write about what they're going to do.* Both have value, but the second one is what builds the bridge between insight and action that TFM requires.

A *TFM-aligned journaling* practice has three specific components, and it takes about eight minutes total. The *first component* is a brief defusion log. Write down one thought that was particularly disturbing or disruptive in the last twenty-four hours. Write it as a labeled thought: "I was having the thought that..." One sentence. You're not analyzing it or working through it. You're practicing the labeling in writing, which reinforces the observer stance in a way that purely mental practice doesn't always achieve. The act of writing the label creates a physical record of the thought as a thought rather than as a fact. That physical record matters more than it might seem.

The *second component* is a brief experiential note. Write one sentence about a difficult feeling you encountered yesterday and how you related to it.

Not how you felt. How you related to the feeling. Did you turn toward it or away from it? Did you fight it or observe it? Did you let it drive your behavior or did you hold it while acting from your values? One sentence, honest and specific. "I felt the anxiety about the presentation and I gave the presentation anyway." Or: "I felt the anxiety about the presentation and I postponed it again." Both are honest. Both are useful information. The honesty is what makes the practice work. A journal that only records your successes is a flattering story. A journal that records both gives you a real map.

The *third component* is a micro-intention. Write one specific, concrete action you'll take today that expresses one of your values. Not a to-do list item. A values-connected behavior. "I'll spend twenty minutes on the project I've been avoiding because I value doing work I'm genuinely proud of." "I'll have the direct conversation with my colleague because I value honest communication." One action. Specific enough to know when you've done it. Connected clearly to a value. This micro-intention does something specific: it sets the day's direction before the day's demands set it for you. You've already decided what matters most. The rest of the day gets filtered through that decision rather than replacing it.

Eight minutes. Defusion log, experiential note, micro-intention. Do this at the same time every day, ideally in the morning before the day begins. The consistency of the time is what builds the habit. The specificity of the three components is what makes it useful rather than just comforting. After two weeks, read back through what you've written. The patterns you'll see in your defusion logs tell you which thoughts are currently consuming the most energy. The patterns in your experiential notes tell you which feelings you're still consistently avoiding. The patterns in your micro-intentions tell you which values you're acting on and which ones you keep writing down without actually doing anything about. That information is your growth map. It's more accurate and more useful than any amount of abstract self-knowledge.

Value-lists work differently from journaling. Where journaling is a daily practice of reflection and intention-setting, a value-list is a standing reference point. It's the document you return to when you've drifted, when you're uncertain about a decision, when the day's demands have crowded out your sense of direction. It's your compass made visible and specific.

A *TFM value-list* isn't a generic list of virtues. It's a personal document with three specific elements. The *first element* is your three to five core values, each written as a behavioral phrase rather than a noun. Not "integrity" but "I say what I actually think even when it's uncomfortable." Not "health" but "I treat my body as something worth taking care of, every day." Not "creativity" but "I make things with real attention and care." These behavioral phrases matter because they point directly toward action. A value stated as a noun is something you believe in. A value stated as a behavior is something you can do today.

The *second element* is one example for each value of a time when you expressed it well. A specific, real memory of yourself acting in alignment with that value. This isn't for nostalgia. It's evidence. When you're having a difficult week and the inner critic is telling you that you always fall short of who you're trying to be, having a specific, written example of a time when you didn't is more useful than any amount of reassurance. It's proof drawn from your own history. It's harder to dismiss than a general affirmation.

The *third element* is one current situation where each value is being tested. Where is your commitment to honest communication being challenged right now? Where is your value of creative engagement being avoided? Where is your commitment to taking care of your health being compromised? This element keeps the value-list alive and relevant rather than becoming a static document you wrote once and never returned to. It connects each value to something real and current in your life.

Update this third element weekly. The values themselves don't change often. The situations where they're being tested change constantly. Keeping the third element current ensures that your value-list is a living tool rather than a completed artifact.

One specific practice that makes your value-list more immediately accessible is what might be called the *values screensaver*. Take your three to five behavioral value phrases and put them as the wallpaper or screensaver on your phone or computer. Not as decoration. As a functional reminder that appears every time you unlock your device. You unlock your phone dozens of times each day. Each time you see your values stated as specific behaviors, you're getting a micro-reminder of your compass. Most of those reminders will pass without conscious registration. Some of them will land at exactly the right moment, when you're about to make a reactive choice and the brief visual cue is enough to create the pause that lets you choose differently instead. The screensaver costs nothing and takes two minutes to set up. The effect, over weeks and months of repeated exposure, is real.

End-of-day reflections are the third structural tool, and they serve a different function from morning journaling. Where the morning practice sets direction, the end-of-day reflection consolidates learning. It's the daily review that turns your lived experience into genuine growth rather than just lived experience that passes without leaving anything useful behind.

A *TFM end-of-day reflection* has four specific questions, and it takes about five minutes. The *first question* is: where did I act from my values today? Name something specific. Even on a difficult day, there's usually something. The conversation you had honestly. The work you stayed with even when it was hard. The moment you turned toward a difficult feeling instead of away from it. Name it specifically. Writing it down reinforces it and builds the evidence base that you're capable of values-aligned behavior even in ordinary, imperfect days.

The *second question* is: where did I drift from my values today? Be honest. Not punishing, but honest. The avoided conversation. The reactive moment. The compulsive phone-checking that replaced the focused work. Name it specifically. The honesty isn't self-punishment. It's information. You can't course-correct what you can't see. The honest acknowledgment, made in the spirit of self-compassion rather than self-criticism, is what makes tomorrow's behavior different from today's.

The *third question is*: what got in the way? Not as an excuse, but as genuine investigation. Was it a specific kind of stress? A particular type of situation? A recurring trigger? Understanding the mechanism of the drift is what allows you to respond to it differently next time. The same drift happening repeatedly under the same conditions isn't a character flaw. It's information about where your practice needs to be focused.

The *fourth question* is: what's one specific thing I'll do differently tomorrow? Not a list of improvements. One thing. Specific and achievable. "I'll use the defusion labeling practice the next time the self-doubt thought arrives before a meeting." "I'll take the two-minute sensory grounding break at 3pm instead of reaching for my phone." "I'll write the micro-intention before I open my email." One thing. The specificity is what makes it actionable rather than aspirational.

Five minutes. Four questions. Every evening before you sleep. The consistency is what makes this a genuine practice rather than an occasional reflection. Over thirty days, the pattern of your answers reveals things about your functioning that you simply can't see without the record. Which values you're consistently acting on and which ones you keep writing about without following through. Which situations reliably pull you off course. Which strategies are actually working and which ones you're doing because they feel productive rather than because they produce results. That information is the foundation of genuine, sustained growth. It's what separates people who understand TFM from people who are actually living it.

There's one more structural practice worth building into your week, and it operates at a slightly longer timescale than the daily tools. *A weekly calibration*, done on Sunday for about fifteen minutes, gives you the perspective that daily reflection can't provide. Where the daily reflection asks what happened today, the weekly calibration asks what pattern is emerging across the week. You're looking for the bigger picture. Which values are getting consistent expression and which ones keep appearing in your drift column? Which situations are repeatedly triggering reactive behavior? Which of your daily practices are you actually doing and which ones have quietly dropped away?

The weekly calibration also includes one forward-looking element: *setting a single focus for the coming week.* Not a goal. A focus. One aspect of your TFM practice that you'll pay particular attention to in the seven days ahead. Maybe it's the defusion check-in that you've been skipping. Maybe it's the presence-based listening practice from Chapter 9 that you want to bring back. Maybe it's the urge surfing technique for a specific compulsive pattern that's been more active lately. One focus. Written down. Returned to at the start of each day that week. The focus doesn't replace your other practices. It sharpens your attention on the area where your growth is most needed right now.

The structure you've been building through this

section, morning journaling, value-lists with a values screensaver, end-of-day reflections, and weekly calibration, isn't complicated. It's consistent. And consistency, applied to the right practices over time, is what turns a set of useful concepts into a genuinely different way of living. The structure holds your direction when motivation fluctuates. It keeps your compass visible when the day's demands would otherwise crowd it out. It turns your lived experience into information you can actually use rather than just experience that passes through you without leaving anything behind.

That's what sustainable psychological flexibility actually looks like in practice. Not a dramatic transformation maintained through sheer force of will. A set of specific, repeatable practices that keep you oriented toward your values even on the ordinary days when nothing particularly inspiring is happening and the internal weather is neither good nor bad, just present, just human, just the normal texture of a life that's actually being lived.

Recap and Action Steps

TFM is not a problem you solve once and move past. It's a practice you deepen continuously. The work you've done across the previous twelve chapters has built real capacity. This chapter has been about making sure that capacity doesn't stay confined to structured practice sessions. It belongs in your morning. In your commute. In your work breaks. In the eight-minute journal entry and the five-minute evening reflection. In the values screensaver that catches you at the right moment on an ordinary Tuesday.

The transcendent life isn't built in dramatic moments of insight. It's built in the small, quiet choices of everyday living. The choice to take three breaths before checking your phone. The choice to put the earbuds away for five minutes on the commute. The choice to name the background thought rather than just live inside it. The choice to write the honest answer in the drift column rather than the comfortable one. These choices are small. Their cumulative effect is not.

The action steps below are your specific, personalized plan for daily practice going forward.

They're not additional practices on top of everything you've already been doing. They're the integration of everything you've built into a sustainable daily structure. Work through them in sequence over the next two weeks to establish the full system, then maintain it as your ongoing practice.

Action step one: Restructure your first ten minutes starting tomorrow morning. Before you check your phone, take three deliberate breaths. Ask yourself out loud: "What do I value most today?" Write the answer and one specific action that expresses that value before noon. Do this every morning for fourteen consecutive days. If you miss a morning, don't restart the count. Just continue. After fourteen days, notice whether the quality of how you enter your days has transformed. Whether you arrive at your work with a direction rather than just a list of demands. That transformation is what you're building.

Action step two: Set up your values screensaver today. Take your three to five behavioral value phrases from your value-list, or write them now if you haven't done this work yet. Put them as the wallpaper on your phone. Do this today, not when you have time. The setup takes two minutes. The effect builds over weeks of repeated exposure. This is the lowest-effort, highest-frequency practice in this entire chapter. Use it.

Action step three: Set three daily defusion check-in alarms on your phone, starting today. Label them "defusion check." Choose three times that are spread across your day, morning, midday, and late afternoon. When each alarm goes off, pause for thirty seconds and ask: "What thought is currently running in the background?" Name it. Label it as a thought. Return to what you were doing. Do this for fourteen consecutive days. After fourteen days, notice whether you're catching the background thought without needing the alarm. That's the awareness the alarm was training.

Action step four: Build the eight-minute morning journaling practice into your routine, starting tomorrow. Defusion log: one thought from the past twenty-four hours, labeled as "I was having the thought that..." Experiential note: one sentence about a difficult feeling and how you related to it. Micro-intention: one specific values-connected action for today. Eight minutes. Same time every morning. Keep a dedicated notebook for this practice, not a general journal. The dedicated notebook becomes a record of your growth that you can review and learn from over time.

Action step five: Begin the five-minute end-of-day reflection tonight. Four questions, written down: where did I act from my values today, where did I drift, what got in the way, and what's one specific thing I'll do differently tomorrow. Keep the same dedicated notebook from action step four. Do this every evening before sleep for the next thirty days. At the end of thirty days, read back through all thirty entries. What you'll find is a genuine map of your functioning, specific, honest, and yours. The patterns it reveals are more valuable than any amount of abstract self-knowledge, because they're drawn from your actual behavior in your actual life. That's where real change lives.

Action step six: Schedule your first weekly calibration for this Sunday. Block fifteen minutes. Review the week's journal entries. Identify the patterns. Set one focus for the coming week. Write it at the top of a fresh page. Return to it each morning as part of your ten-minute morning practice. Do this every Sunday going forward. The weekly calibration is what keeps the daily practices from drifting into ritual without substance. It's the meta-level review that ensures you're not just doing the practices but actually learning from them.

These six action steps form a complete daily and weekly structure. They're specific enough to be actionable, brief enough to be sustainable, and connected enough to your values that they don't require motivation to maintain. They require only the decision, made once and renewed daily, to show up for the practice regardless of how you feel about it on any given morning.

That decision, made consistently over months, is what the transcendent life is actually built from. Not from dramatic breakthroughs or perfect weeks or the days when everything aligns and the practice feels meaningful and alive. From the ordinary days too. The flat ones. The resistant ones. The ones where the defusion check-in feels mechanical and the morning journal feels like going through the motions. Those days count just as much as the inspired ones. They might count more, because showing up on those days is what builds the capacity that makes transcendent functioning reliable rather than occasional.

You've covered the full architecture of the

Transcendent Functioning Model across these thirteen chapters. The concepts, the mechanisms, the clinical applications, the moment-to-moment practices, and now the daily structure that holds all of it together over time. What remains is simply the living of it. Imperfect, continuous, and genuinely yours.

Chapter Fourteen

The Future of Transcendent Functioning

You've built something real. Across thirteen chapters, you've worked through the mechanics of operating above your emotional state. You've practiced defusion, expanded your tolerance for discomfort, loosened your grip on rigid outcomes, and learned to act from your values even when your internal world isn't cooperating. That's not small work. And it doesn't stop here.

This chapter is about what comes next. Not just for you personally, but for the larger world that the principles you've been practicing are beginning to touch. TFM didn't emerge in a vacuum. It sits at the intersection of decades of psychological research, clinical practice, and a growing recognition that the old model of mental health, focused almost entirely on reducing what's wrong, can't take us where we actually need to go. The question this chapter asks is a bigger one: what happens when these principles scale beyond the individual? What does a world look like when more people are operating from values rather than from fear?

That question isn't abstract. It has direct, practical implications for how organizations function, how schools educate, how communities hold together under pressure. And it has implications for your brain, specifically, in ways that science is only beginning to fully map.

Expanding the Framework

The principles you've been working with in this book didn't stay contained to therapy offices. They've been moving outward, into workplaces, schools, and communities, because the problems they address aren't clinical problems. They're human problems. Fragmented attention. Reactive decision-making. The gap between what people know matters and what they actually do. These patterns show up everywhere people gather under pressure.

Consider what reactive functioning looks like at the organizational level. A team where decisions get made based on whoever is most emotionally forceful in the room. A company culture where people avoid raising real problems because the anxiety around conflict is too high. A leadership structure where the person at the top is so attached to a specific outcome that they can't adapt when conditions change. These aren't unusual scenarios. They're the norm in most organizations. And the cost isn't just human wellbeing. It's performance, innovation, and long-term survival.

Regulated functioning at the organizational level looks slightly better. There are processes. There are conflict resolution protocols. There are leadership development programs that teach emotional intelligence and self-regulation. These are real improvements over pure reactivity. But they carry the same limitation that individual regulation carries: they require constant effort and they tend to collapse under high-stakes pressure, which is exactly when they're most needed.

What would transcendent functioning look like in an organization? It would look like a team that can hold genuine disagreement without it becoming personal. A culture where difficult feedback is given and received as information rather than threat. A leadership style that stays oriented toward the organization's core values even when the external environment is chaotic.

Decision-making that's driven by what the organization actually stands for rather than by the anxiety of the moment. These aren't utopian fantasies. They're the natural result of applying TFM principles at scale.

Think about what this means practically. If you're in a leadership position, the most important thing you can do for your team's psychological functioning is model the exact capacities this book has been building. When you defuse from a threatening thought in a meeting rather than reacting to it, you're demonstrating that it's possible. When you acknowledge uncertainty honestly instead of projecting false confidence, you're creating permission for others to do the same. When you make a decision based on what the organization values rather than what feels safest in the moment, you're showing your team what value-driven action looks like at scale. Leadership, in this model, isn't about having the right answers. It's about demonstrating the right relationship to difficulty.

The education context is where these principles have perhaps the most significant long-term impact. Children and adolescents are in the process of forming their fundamental relationship to their own internal experience. The patterns they develop during those years, whether they learn to avoid discomfort or to hold it, whether they learn to be controlled by their emotional states or to act from their values in their presence, shape decades of subsequent functioning. Most educational systems, even well-intentioned ones, teach primarily at the reactive and regulated levels. They teach emotional management. They don't teach psychological flexibility. They teach coping. They don't teach transcendent functioning.

What would it look like to teach these principles in schools? Not as a separate class, but woven into the fabric of how learning happens. Teaching students to notice when a thought is creating avoidance rather than just acting on the avoidance. Helping them identify what they value about their learning rather than just what grade they're trying to achieve. Building their capacity to stay present with the discomfort of not knowing rather than immediately seeking the comfort of a quick answer. These aren't additions to the curriculum. They're a different quality of attention brought to everything that's already there.

Imagine a hypothetical 16-year-old named Sam who has been struggling with test anxiety for two years. Every exam period, the anxiety spikes, the avoidance kicks in, and the studying that should happen doesn't. Sam isn't lazy. Sam is reactive. The anxiety arrives, and the behavior follows the anxiety rather than Sam's actual values around learning and achievement. A school environment that teaches TFM principles would give Sam specific tools: the ability to notice the anxiety as a feeling rather than a command, the capacity to stay with the discomfort of studying even when the anxiety is present, and the understanding that the anxiety before an exam is a signal that the exam matters, not evidence that failure is certain. Those tools don't just help Sam pass the next test. They change Sam's fundamental relationship to difficulty, which carries forward into every subsequent challenge.

Community building is the third domain where TFM principles have significant implications, and it's the one that's hardest to operationalize but perhaps most important. Communities under stress, whether that stress is economic, political, or social, tend to collapse into reactive functioning at the collective level. People organize around fear. Decision-making becomes dominated by whoever can generate the most anxiety in others. Differences that could be navigated become threats that must be eliminated. The psychological mechanisms that operate in individuals under stress operate in groups too, and they produce the same narrowing, the same defensiveness, the same inability to act from shared values when the emotional pressure is high enough.

A community that has developed collective psychological flexibility looks different. People can hold disagreement without it becoming existential. Difficult conversations happen because they're valued rather than avoided because they're uncomfortable. Decisions get made based on what the community actually cares about rather than what generates the least immediate conflict. This isn't idealism. It's the natural result of enough individuals within a community developing the capacities this book has been building. Individual psychological flexibility aggregates. It becomes cultural. And culture, once established, shapes how the next generation learns to relate to difficulty.

Here's what this means for you specifically, right now, in your actual life. You don't need to wait for organizations or schools or communities to adopt TFM principles before you can contribute to that larger transformation. You're already contributing to it through how you show up. Every time you respond to a difficult situation from your values rather than from your anxiety, you're modeling something for everyone around you. Every time you have the honest conversation instead of the comfortable one, you're demonstrating that it's possible. Every time you stay present with uncertainty rather than demanding premature resolution, you're showing the people in your life what psychological flexibility looks like in practice.

The ripple effect is real. It's not dramatic. It doesn't announce itself. But it's there.

To bring value-driven action into your workplace or community in a concrete way, start with one specific and small commitment. Identify one situation in your professional or community life where reactive functioning is currently running the show. A meeting that always devolves into defensiveness. A community conversation that never gets past the surface because the real disagreements feel too risky. A team dynamic where important problems go unspoken because the culture doesn't feel safe enough for honesty. Pick one. Then identify one specific, value-driven action you can take in that situation this week. Not a system change. Not a culture overhaul. One action, aligned with what you actually value, taken in the presence of whatever discomfort it produces. That one action is how the larger transformation begins. Always through the individual. Always through the specific. Always through the choice made in a real moment rather than the intention held in the abstract.

The Neurobiology of Transcendence

The practices in this book aren't just psychologically useful. They're physically changing your brain. That's not a metaphor. It's a description of what the emerging neuroscience of psychological flexibility is beginning to map with increasing precision. Understanding what's happening at the neural level when you practice defusion, experiential expansion, and value-driven action gives you something important: the knowledge that the work you're doing has a tangible, physical substrate. You're not just thinking differently. You're literally building a different brain.

Start with the threat response system, because it's the foundation of everything reactive functioning runs on. The amygdala, which you encountered earlier, is your brain's primary threat detector. It fires fast, before your conscious mind has time to weigh in, and it produces the cascade of physiological responses, elevated heart rate, narrowed attention, heightened muscle tension, that prepare you to fight, flee, or freeze. This system is ancient, essential, and, in the modern context, frequently misfiring. It treats the anxiety before a difficult conversation with the same urgency it would treat a physical threat. And when it fires, it temporarily suppresses activity in the prefrontal cortex, which is the part of your brain responsible for deliberate, values-based decision-making.

That suppression is the neurological basis of reactive functioning. The amygdala is loud. The prefrontal cortex goes quiet. Your behavior follows the amygdala rather than your values, not because you're weak or undisciplined, but because that's what happens when the threat response hijacks the system. This is why insight alone doesn't change reactive behavior. You can understand the pattern completely and still run it, because understanding happens in the prefrontal cortex and the amygdala doesn't consult it when it's alarmed.

The practices in this book work, in part, by

changing the relationship between these two systems. Mindfulness-based practices, which underpin much of the TFM approach, have been shown in neuroimaging research to reduce amygdala reactivity over time. A landmark study by Sara Lazar at Harvard Medical School found that experienced meditators showed measurably thicker cortical regions in areas associated with attention, interoception, and sensory processing, and reduced amygdala gray matter density compared to non-meditators. The brain changes in response to practice. The threat response system becomes less hair-trigger. The prefrontal cortex becomes more accessible even under stress.

Cognitive defusion, the practice you've been building since Chapter 2, has its own neural signature. When you label a thought as a thought rather than experiencing it as reality, you're engaging a process that neuroscientists sometimes call affect labeling. Research by Matthew Lieberman at UCLA has shown that affect labeling, putting feelings and thoughts into words, reduces activity in the amygdala and increases activity in the right ventrolateral prefrontal cortex. In plain terms: naming what's happening in your mind creates measurable distance between the emotional experience and the behavioral response. The gap you've been practicing creating isn't just a psychological phenomenon. It's a neural one. You're literally activating a different part of your brain when you say "I'm having the thought that..." rather than simply being inside the thought.

The observing self, which appeared in Chapter 3 and has been a recurring concept throughout this book, has a neurological correlate that's worth understanding. The *default mode network*, or DMN, is a set of brain regions that become active when you're not focused on the external world. It's associated with self-referential thinking, mind-wandering, and the kind of rumination that keeps reactive functioning in place. When you're caught in a worry spiral or a self-critical loop, your DMN is highly active. When you transformation to the observer stance, something different happens. Research suggests that mindfulness practice and the kind of present-moment contact that TFM builds are associated with reduced DMN activity and increased activity in regions associated with present-moment sensory awareness. You're literally transformationing which network is running the show.

The neural correlates of value-driven action are perhaps the most compelling piece of the neuroscientific picture. When you act in alignment with your values, particularly when you do so in the presence of discomfort rather than waiting for the discomfort to clear, you're engaging the prefrontal cortex in a way that builds its capacity over time. This is the neural basis of what psychologists call ego strength, the capacity to override immediate impulses in service of longer-term values. Research on self-regulation consistently shows that this capacity is trainable. It's not fixed. The prefrontal cortex responds to use the way muscles respond to exercise. The more you practice deliberate, values-based decision-making under conditions of emotional pressure, the more accessible that capacity becomes the next time pressure arrives.

There's a specific neurological mechanism worth naming here because it explains something that many people find confusing about their own experience. When you first start practicing TFM principles, the practices often feel effortful and somewhat artificial. Labeling thoughts, turning toward discomfort, acting from values when your emotional state is pushing in a different direction, these things require conscious attention and deliberate choice. They don't feel natural yet. That's because they're being processed primarily in the prefrontal cortex, which is slower and more effortful than the automatic systems. But with repetition, something changes. The practices begin to be processed in different neural circuits, ones associated with habit and automaticity. The defusion that once required conscious effort starts happening faster, more naturally, with less deliberate attention. This is neuroplasticity in action. The brain is reorganizing itself around the patterns you're practicing.

This reorganization has a name in the neuroscience literature: *experience-dependent plasticity*. Your brain changes in response to what you repeatedly do and attend to. This is both a warning and an opportunity. The warning: if you repeatedly practice avoidance, your brain gets better at avoidance. The threat response becomes more sensitive. The prefrontal cortex becomes less accessible under pressure. The reactive patterns become more automatic. The opportunity: if you repeatedly practice the TFM principles, your brain gets better at them too. Defusion becomes more accessible. Tolerance for discomfort widens. Value-driven action becomes more automatic. The transcendent functioning that currently requires deliberate effort gradually becomes your default operating mode.

The practical implication of all this neuroscience is straightforward and important. Consistency matters more than intensity. A brief daily practice that you actually do produces more lasting neural change than an intensive practice you do occasionally. The brain changes through repetition, not through dramatic single experiences. This is why the daily structure from Chapter 13, the morning journaling, the defusion check-ins, the end-of-day reflection, is so important. These aren't just organizational tools. They're the repeated activations that drive the neural reorganization that makes transcendent functioning durable.

Your brain is not fixed. The patterns you've been running, the reactive loops, the avoidance cycles, the fused relationship with your own thoughts, these were learned. They were built through repetition in your history. And they can be rebuilt through repetition in your present. Every time you practice defusion, you're strengthening the neural pathway that makes defusion available. Every time you turn toward discomfort instead of away from it, you're building the neural architecture of a wider tolerance window. Every time you act from your values in the presence of a difficult internal state, you're reinforcing the prefrontal cortex's capacity to stay online under pressure.

The science doesn't just validate the practice. It explains why the practice works, which makes it easier to stay with on the days when it doesn't feel like it's working. The neural change is happening whether you can feel it or not. The brain is adapting to what you're repeatedly doing. The question is only whether what you're repeatedly doing is building the architecture of transcendent functioning or the architecture of reactive avoidance. Both are options. Both are the result of practice. Only one of them is the result of conscious choice.

Here are three specific practices grounded in the neuroscience described above, designed to be added to the daily structure you built in Chapter 13 or used as standalone tools when the existing practices need refreshing.

The first is the affect labeling practice for emotional intensity. When you notice a strong emotional state arising, whether it's anxiety, frustration, shame, or overwhelm, pause and write or say out loud a complete description of what's happening: "I'm noticing [emotion name] right now. It feels like [physical description] in my [body location]." The specificity matters. "I'm anxious" is less neurologically effective than "I'm noticing anxiety right now. It feels like a tight band across my chest." The more specific the labeling, the more reliably it activates the affect labeling circuit that reduces amygdala activity. Do this every time emotional intensity rises above a seven out of ten for the next two weeks. Write the descriptions down. After two weeks, notice whether the labeling is becoming more automatic and whether the emotional intensity drops more quickly when you use it.

The second practice is a brief daily default mode network interruption. Once each day, at a time when you notice your mind has been wandering or caught in rumination, do a thirty-second sensory grounding. Name five things you can see right now. Four things you can physically feel. Three things you can hear. Two things you can smell. One thing you can taste. This sequence pulls your attention from the self-referential DMN activity into present-moment sensory awareness, which activates different neural circuits. It's brief enough to do anywhere and effective enough to produce a measurable transformation in attentional quality. Use it whenever you catch yourself in a rumination loop rather than waiting for a scheduled practice time.

The third practice is what might be called a prefrontal priming exercise, done before any high-stakes situation where you know reactive functioning is likely to show up. Two to three minutes before a difficult meeting, a challenging conversation, or any situation that typically triggers your reactive patterns, do this sequence. Sit quietly. Take five slow breaths, making the exhale longer than the inhale. This activates the parasympathetic nervous system and begins to down-regulate the amygdala before the situation begins. Then identify your relevant value for this specific situation in one sentence: "What I care about most here is [specific value]." Say it out loud if you can. Then ask: "What's one thing I can do in the next few minutes that expresses that value?" Answer it. Write it if there's time. This sequence takes less than three minutes and has a specific neurological function: you're priming the prefrontal cortex before the amygdala has a chance to take over. You're setting your values as the operating system before the emotional pressure arrives. The situations that used to reliably produce reactive behavior become more navigable because you've given your prefrontal cortex a head start.

Recap and Action Steps

This chapter has covered a lot of ground, and it's worth pulling the threads together clearly before you close this book and carry what you've built into your actual life.

The Transcendent Functioning Model is bigger than any individual's personal growth. The principles you've been practicing, the capacity to hold difficult internal experience without being controlled by it, to act from values under pressure, to observe your thoughts rather than being inside them, these principles apply wherever human beings gather under stress. In organizations, they produce cultures where real problems get named and addressed rather than avoided. In schools, they give young people a fundamentally different relationship to difficulty. In communities, they create the conditions for genuine dialogue rather than reactive conflict. The work you've done on yourself is a contribution to all of that, because the people around you are shaped by how you show up, and how you show up is shaped by what you've built inside.

The neuroscience behind these practices is real

and specific. Your brain is changing in response to what you repeatedly do. The amygdala becomes less reactive with consistent mindfulness-based practice. The prefrontal cortex becomes more accessible under pressure with repeated value-driven action. The defusion skills become more automatic with daily practice. The neural reorganization is happening whether you can feel it or not. The consistency of your practice is what determines its depth and durability.

The movement toward human flourishing that TFM represents isn't a utopian idea. It's a direction. A direction made real through individual choices, made daily, in ordinary moments, by people who have decided that operating above their emotional noise is worth the effort of building the capacity to do so. You're one of those people now. The question isn't whether you have the tools. You do. The question is only whether you'll use them.

The action steps below are your final set. They're designed to consolidate everything from this chapter and point you toward what comes next.

Action step one: Identify one specific way you'll bring value-driven action into your

workplace or community this week. Be concrete. Not "I'll try to be more values-driven at work" but "In Tuesday's team meeting, when the conversation gets defensive, I'll name what I value about the outcome we're trying to reach and ask one question that redirects toward that." Write it down. Treat it as a commitment. After the situation, write two sentences about what happened. Did the value-driven action change the quality of the interaction? Did it change anything for the people around you? That record is your evidence that the principles extend beyond your internal world into the shared world you inhabit with others.

Action step two: Add the affect labeling practice to your existing toolkit for the next two weeks. Every time emotional intensity rises above a seven out of ten, write or say the complete description: "I'm noticing [emotion] right now. It feels like [physical description] in [body location]." Do this every time, not occasionally. After two weeks, notice whether the labeling is becoming more automatic. Whether the emotional intensity drops more quickly when you use it. Whether you're catching the emotion earlier, before it reaches the peak that makes reactive behavior most likely. Write one sentence summarizing what you noticed. That sentence is your data point on whether the practice is producing the neural effect it's designed to produce.

Action step three: Use the prefrontal priming sequence before one high-stakes situation this week. Identify the situation in advance. Two to three minutes before it begins, do the full sequence: five slow breaths with extended exhale, identify your relevant value in one sentence, ask and answer what one action expresses that value in this situation. Notice what's different about how you enter the situation compared to how you'd normally enter it. Write one sentence afterward about what you observed. The priming won't make the situation easy. It will make your prefrontal cortex more available when you need it. That's the specific, neurological outcome you're building toward.

Action step four: Write a brief personal statement about what TFM means for your life going forward. Not a summary of the book. A personal statement about where you've come from and where you're headed. What was your primary stuck pattern when you started reading? What's different now, even if imperfectly? What's the most important thing you've built across these fourteen chapters? And what's the one practice you're most committed to maintaining going forward? Write it in your journal. Read it once a month. Let it evolve as you do. This statement isn't a final destination. It's a marker of where you are right now, which is further along than where you were, and not yet as far as you'll be.

The science is real. The practices are specific. The brain is changing. And the life you're building, one small, consistent, values-driven choice at a time, is already different from the one you were living before you began.

Chapter Fifteen

Sustaining the Journey: A Lifelong Practice

You've covered a lot of ground. From understanding what reactive functioning actually costs you, to building the specific skills of defusion, experiential expansion, and value-driven action, to seeing how those skills apply under the real pressure of anxiety, depression, trauma, and compulsive patterns. You've built something real across these pages. And now comes the question that determines whether any of it actually holds.

What happens next?

Not next week, when the motivation from finishing a book is still fresh. Not next month, when the practices are still relatively new and the novelty is carrying some of the load. What happens in year two? Year three? What happens when you've had a genuinely difficult stretch, when the practices have slipped, when the old patterns have come back louder than expected, and the version of yourself that started this book feels very far away?

That's what this final chapter is about. Not the beginning of the work, *but the continuation of it.*

The Dynamic Nature of Becoming

There's a version of personal growth that a lot of people carry around without examining it. It goes something like this: you learn what you need to learn, you do the work, you change, and then you're changed. You arrive. The difficult version of yourself is replaced by the better one, and the better one stays. Growth, in this version, is a destination. A before and an after. A problem solved.

That version is wrong. And believing it causes more unnecessary suffering than almost any other misconception about how change actually works.

Becoming is not a destination. It's a direction. You don't arrive at transcendent functioning and then maintain it effortlessly for the rest of your life. You practice it, imperfectly, continuously, with periods of real progress followed by periods of regression followed by return. The regression isn't evidence that the growth wasn't real. It's evidence that you're human, doing something genuinely difficult, in a world that doesn't always cooperate with your best intentions.

The most important reframe in this entire chapter is this: the goal was never to become a person who doesn't struggle. The goal was to become a person who relates to struggle differently. And that relationship is something you practice, not something you achieve once and possess permanently.

Low motivation periods are part of this. They're not aberrations. They're not signs that the whole system has failed. They're the ordinary texture of a life that's actually being lived by a human nervous system with real limits. There will be weeks where the morning journaling feels mechanical. Weeks where the defusion practice feels like going through motions. Weeks where the values you spent time clarifying feel distant and abstract. Those weeks don't mean the practice isn't working. They mean you're in a low-energy phase of a long cycle, and the right response isn't to diagnose yourself as having failed. It's to do the smallest possible version of the practice and keep going.

Think about what regression actually looks like in practice. It's rarely dramatic. It's not usually a single catastrophic collapse back to your worst patterns. It's more subtle than that. The phone gets checked before the three morning breaths. The defusion check-in gets skipped for a few days, then a week, then it's just gone. The end-of-day reflection stops happening because you're tired and it doesn't feel urgent. The reactive response comes out in a conversation and you notice it only afterward. None of these things are catastrophic. But they accumulate. And if you don't have a clear way of noticing the accumulation and returning without drama, the drift becomes the new normal.

The self-correction practice from Chapter 5 applies here in its fullest form. When you notice you've drifted, the move is always the same. Name what happened specifically. Identify what got in the way. Offer yourself the honest, compassionate acknowledgment from Chapter 10. Take one small, concrete action today that expresses the value you drifted from. Not a grand re-commitment. Not a new system. One action. That action is the return. And the return, made without drama, without self-punishment, and without the requirement that it feel meaningful in the moment, is the most important skill in this entire book.

Consider a hypothetical scenario: someone like Kenji, a 33-year-old software developer who worked seriously with TFM principles for about eight months, made genuine progress, and then went through a period of significant personal stress that pulled him almost entirely back into reactive patterns. He stopped the practices. He started avoiding the difficult conversations again. He found himself back in the familiar loop of insight, motivation, inconsistency, and frustration. What he didn't have, at that point, was the understanding that this cycle wasn't proof that the previous eight months had been wasted. It was proof that he was a human being under significant stress, and that the practices needed to be returned to, not restarted from scratch. When he finally came back, he didn't begin at chapter one. He began with the smallest possible action: one morning of three breaths and one values question. That was enough. The return doesn't require a dramatic recommitment. It just requires the next small step.

Handling periods of low motivation requires a specific strategy that's different from what works during high-motivation periods. When motivation is high, ambitious practices are sustainable. When motivation is low, ambitious practices become another thing to fail at. The strategy for low-motivation periods is radical reduction. Not abandonment. Reduction. What's the absolute smallest version of this practice that I can actually do today? Not the ideal version. The minimum viable version. Three breaths instead of ten minutes of journaling. One defusion label instead of a full visualization practice. One sentence of honest reflection instead of four questions. The minimum viable version keeps the thread intact. It keeps you in contact with the practice even when the practice can't be full. And it keeps the return, when energy comes back, much shorter and less effortful than if you'd stopped completely.

There's a deeper truth underneath all of this that's worth stating plainly. The goal of sustained practice isn't to never fall back. It's to shorten the time between falling back and returning. A person who practiced TFM for three years and has developed genuine psychological flexibility doesn't never have reactive weeks. They notice the reactive week sooner, return to their values faster, and don't make the regression mean something catastrophic about their capacity for growth. That's the real measure of progress. Not the absence of difficult periods. The quality of how you move through them and come back.

Perfection was never the standard. Showing up was always the standard. Showing up imperfectly, consistently, over time. That's what the practice is. That's what becoming actually looks like from the inside.

Evolving Your Values

The values you identified when you started this work were real. They were genuinely yours. And they were also a snapshot. A picture of what mattered most to you at a particular moment in your life, with the particular level of self-knowledge you had at that time, filtered through the particular experiences you'd had up to that point. Those values are a starting point, not a final answer.

Values evolve. Not because you were wrong about them before. Because you grow, your understanding deepens, your circumstances change, and what you're capable of caring about expands. The person who identified "honest communication" as a core value at twenty-eight might find, at thirty-five, that the value has deepened into something more nuanced. It's not just honesty now. It's honest presence. The willingness to be genuinely seen, not just to say true things. The evolution isn't a correction. It's a refinement. The same value, understood more fully.

There's also a category of values evolution that's more substantial than refinement. Sometimes life changes in ways that genuinely transformation what matters most. The birth of a child. The death of someone central to your life. A career change that takes you somewhere you didn't expect. A health challenge that reorganizes your priorities in ways you couldn't have anticipated. These experiences don't just add to your values. They can rearrange them. What mattered most before might still matter, but it might matter differently. And something that felt peripheral might move to the center in a way that changes everything about how you engage with your daily life.

The risk of treating your values as fixed is that you end up living by a compass that's pointing somewhere you've already been. You keep organizing your life around what mattered at a previous chapter of your story, without noticing that the story has moved on. The practices feel hollow because they're expressing values that no longer quite fit. The intentional actions feel mechanical because they're connected to a version of what matters that's slightly out of date. The whole system starts to feel like you're going through motions rather than genuinely living.

The solution is to treat your values as a living document rather than a settled one. This doesn't mean changing them every few months based on whatever you're currently excited about. That would be chasing novelty rather than clarifying depth. It means returning to the values clarification work from Chapter 5 at meaningful intervals and asking honestly: is this still true? Is this still the most accurate description of what I care about? Is there something underneath this value that I can see more clearly now than I could before?

A specific practice for this is what might be called *the annual values audit*. Once each year, ideally around a natural transition point like the beginning of a new year, a birthday, or another personally significant marker, set aside about an hour and return to the four questions from Chapter 5. Think about when you felt most genuinely yourself in the past year. Think about what made you most angry or troubled. Think about what you'd still choose if all external expectations were removed. Think about the qualities you want to have expressed consistently when you look back. Write your answers. Then compare them to the behavioral value phrases you've been working with. Where are they consistent? Where have they evolved? Where is there something new that needs to be named?

Update your value-list based on what you find. Not wholesale. With attention to what's deepened, what's transformationed, and what's genuinely new. Then update the values screensaver. Update the micro-intentions in your morning journal. Let the evolved understanding of your values flow through the entire daily structure you've built.

There's a subtlety here that's worth naming carefully. *Values evolution isn't the same as values abandonment.* And it's not the same as values drift, where you gradually stop acting on what you care about because life got busy or the practices slipped. *Values abandonment is conscious and often comes from genuine growth*, you've realized that something you thought you valued was actually driven by fear or external expectation rather than genuine care. *Values drift is unconscious and usually comes from avoidance.* The annual audit helps you distinguish between the two. When you sit down with honest attention and ask "is this still true?", you can usually feel the difference between a value that's genuinely evolved and a value that you've simply been too busy or too avoidant to act on. The first deserves updating. The second deserves renewed commitment.

Your purpose is a living thing. Not a mission statement you wrote once and laminated. Not a destination you're heading toward. A living commitment that breathes and changes as you do. The people who find the deepest satisfaction in their lives aren't the ones who figured out their purpose at twenty-five and never deviated from it. They're the ones who stayed in ongoing, honest conversation with what mattered to them, updated their understanding as they grew, and kept aligning their behavior with that evolving understanding across decades of living. That ongoing conversation is what a committed life actually looks like from the inside.

One more practice worth building into your relationship with your values: *share them.* Not publicly, necessarily, and not as performance. But with one or two people who know you well and care about your growth. Tell them what you value and why. Tell them when you feel like you're living it and when you feel like you're not. Ask them what they observe. The external perspective of someone who knows you and isn't invested in your self-image is one of the most useful mirrors available. It catches the blind spots that your own self-assessment misses. It notices when the values you're espousing and the life you're actually living have drifted further apart than you've acknowledged. And it offers the particular kind of accountability that only genuine relationship can provide: the accountability that comes not from judgment but from being genuinely known.

Your values are your compass. Keep it calibrated. Keep it honest. Keep it alive.

The Final Call to Action

You've almost reached the end of this book. That's worth pausing to acknowledge, not because finishing a book is an achievement in itself, but because what you've built across these pages is real. The understanding isn't just intellectual. You've practiced. You've applied. You've returned after drifting. You've built, however imperfectly, a different relationship to your own internal experience. That's not nothing. That's the foundation of everything.

But a foundation is only as valuable as what you build on it. And what you build on it happens in the ordinary moments of your actual life. Not in the reading. In the doing. In the Tuesday afternoon when the reactive pattern shows up and you notice it a half-second earlier than you would have six months ago. In the conversation where you feel the defensive response rising and you choose the honest one instead. In the morning where the practice feels mechanical and you do the minimum viable version anyway, because keeping the thread is more important than doing it perfectly. In the setback where the old self-critical voice arrives and you offer yourself the honest, compassionate acknowledgment rather than the verdict.

Every single moment is an opportunity to practice what you've built. Not in a pressured way. Not with the expectation that you'll do it right every time. But with the recognition that the practice is always available, always possible, and always worth returning to. The moment you notice you've drifted is already the beginning of the return. The noticing itself is a skill. And it's a skill you've been building throughout every chapter of this book.

The world you're going to live in after closing this book isn't going to cooperate perfectly with your best intentions. It's going to be demanding and unpredictable and sometimes genuinely hard. The people around you aren't always going to make it easy to operate from your values. The circumstances you find yourself in aren't always going to be the ones that bring out your best. That's not a problem with the world. That's the world. And operating above your emotions doesn't mean operating in spite of the world. It means operating fully within it, with all its difficulty and complexity, guided by something more durable than the weather of any given day.

You already know how to do this. You've been building the capacity across every chapter. The defusion skills are yours. The expanded tolerance is yours. The looser grip on rigid conditions is yours. The commitment to value-driven action is yours. The self-compassion that makes returning possible without drama is yours. These aren't borrowed tools you're holding temporarily. They're capacities you've developed. They belong to you now in the way that any practiced skill belongs to the person who practiced it.

What remains is simply the living of it.

Imperfect, continuous, honest, and genuinely yours.

The storms don't stop. The difficult thoughts don't permanently disappear. The anxiety, the self-doubt, the grief, the frustration, these are features of a human life fully lived, and no honest framework promises their elimination. What changes, through the work you've done, is your relationship to all of it. You stop being someone who is managed by their internal experience and become someone who can feel everything and still choose. That's not a small transformation. It's the transformation that makes everything else in your life more possible.

Keep practicing. Keep returning. Keep the compass calibrated. That's enough. That's always been enough.

Recap and Action Steps

This final chapter has covered three connected ideas. The dynamic nature of becoming, which means accepting that growth is continuous and non-linear, that regression is part of the process rather than evidence of failure, and that the quality of your return matters more than the prevention of the drift. The evolution of your values, which means treating your inner compass as a living document that deepens and refines as you grow, rather than a fixed statement you made once and must maintain unchanged. And the ongoing invitation to practice, which means recognizing that every ordinary moment is an opportunity to express what you've built, and that the practice continues as long as you do.

The action steps below are your closing commitments. They're fewer in number than previous chapters because depth matters more than breadth here. Work through them slowly and honestly.

Action step one: Write a letter to your future self. Not a short note. A real letter. Address it to yourself one year from now. In the letter, describe specifically what you value most right now and why. Describe the patterns you've been working to change and the progress you've made, honestly, without inflation or minimization. Describe what you're committing to in the year ahead, not in terms of goals but in terms of how you want to show up, what practices you're committing to maintaining, and what you'll do when you drift.

Write about what you want the person reading this letter in a year to have built, experienced, and become. Seal it. Date it. Put it somewhere you'll find it in twelve months. When you open it, use it as the starting point for your annual values audit. The letter creates a specific, personal record of where you are right now, which makes the evolution of the next year visible and meaningful rather than vague and untracked.

Action step two: Schedule your first annual values audit. Pick a date within the next thirty days that feels like a natural marker. Your birthday. The first of a new month. A personally significant anniversary. Block ninety minutes. Return to the four values clarification questions from Chapter 5. Write full answers. Compare them to the behavioral value phrases you've been working with. Update what needs updating. Rewrite your value-list with the evolved understanding. Update your values screensaver. This audit isn't a sign that your previous values were wrong. It's evidence that you're growing. Do it every year from this point forward. Mark it in your calendar now, before you close this book.

Action step three: Design your minimum viable practice. Sit down with a pen and paper and answer this question: if my life became genuinely overwhelming and I could only maintain the smallest possible version of my TFM practice, what would that look like? Be specific. Not "I'd try to stay mindful" but "I'd do three morning breaths, one defusion label when I notice a sticky thought, and one sentence of honest reflection before sleep." Write it down. Keep it somewhere accessible. This is your floor. The version of practice that keeps the thread intact even when everything else is under pressure. Having it written in advance means you don't have to decide in the middle of a difficult period what the minimum looks like. The decision has already been made. The only question is whether you do it.

Action step four: Tell one person what you've committed to. Choose someone who knows you well and genuinely cares about your growth. Tell them specifically what you value, what you've been working to change, and what you're committing to going forward. Ask them to check in with you in three months. Not to hold you accountable in a punishing way. To be curious about how it's going. This single act of honest sharing does two things simultaneously. It makes your commitment more real by giving it a witness. And it begins to extend the principles of this book into your relationships,which is where they ultimately need to live to have their full effect.

The work doesn't end here. It continues in the ordinary moments of your actual life, in every choice made from your values rather than your anxiety, in every return made without drama after a drift, in every moment of genuine presence offered to the people and work and experiences that matter most to you. That's what a transcendent life actually looks like. Not a peak state. A practice. Yours, continuously, for as long as you choose to keep showing up for it.

Conclusion

You made it here. Not just to the end of a book, but through a genuine restructuring of how you relate to your own mind. That's worth acknowledging before anything else.

What you've built across these pages isn't a collection of techniques you picked up and might use someday. It's a different architecture. A different way of processing the difficulty, the noise, the self-doubt, and the chaos that are simply part of being an ambitious, awake, fully alive human being. The work was real. The transformation, however imperfect and ongoing, is real too.

This conclusion isn't a summary in the traditional sense. It's a landing point. A place to stand, look back at where you've come from, look forward at where you're headed, and carry the most essential pieces of this work clearly in your hands as you walk back into your actual life.

Summarizing the Transcendent Path

The core idea running through every chapter of this book is simple enough to say in one sentence, but it takes a lifetime to fully live. You don't have to wait for your internal world to calm down before you can show up fully for your life. That's it. That's the whole thing.

Everything else has been the unpacking of that idea. The defusion work showed you that your thoughts aren't facts. They're mental events, produced automatically by a brain doing its best to keep you safe, and they don't have to be the deciding factor in what you do next. The experiential expansion work showed you that difficult feelings don't have to be escaped. They can be held, observed, and allowed to move through you rather than being fought into a corner where they grow stronger. The attachment reduction work showed you that the conditions you've been requiring before you'll allow yourself to function fully, the readiness, the certainty, the right emotional state, are not actually requirements. They're habits of mind that can be loosened without losing what matters.

And the intentional action work showed you what to do with all of that space.

The three levels of functioning gave you a map. Reactive functioning, where your internal states run the show and your behavior is essentially a direct output of whatever feeling is loudest. Regulated functioning, where you've learned to manage the internal weather skillfully but find yourself always bracing, always monitoring, always one difficult emotion away from needing to intervene. And transcendent functioning, where your values drive your choices, the difficult feelings are present and acknowledged and no longer in charge, and your execution stays consistent regardless of what your internal world is doing on any given day.

Most people spend their entire lives between the first two levels. Not because they lack intelligence or desire, but because nobody ever showed them there was a third option. This book showed you the third option. More importantly, it gave you the specific practices to actually get there and stay there, imperfectly, continuously, for real.

True peace, the kind that actually holds, doesn't come from the absence of struggle. It comes from alignment. From the sense that what you're doing, how you're showing up, the choices you're making, these things are genuinely connected to what you value at the deepest level. When that alignment is present, the storms don't disappear. They just stop being the deciding factor. You can feel the anxiety and still walk into the room. You can feel the self-doubt and still start the work. You can feel the grief and still show up for the people who need you. That's not invincibility. That's freedom. And it's available to you right now, in the life you're actually living, not in some future version of it where everything is finally sorted out.

The gap between who you know you can be and how you've been showing up isn't a character flaw. It's a structural problem. And structural problems have structural solutions. The architecture you've been building across these chapters is that solution. Not a perfect one. A real one.

A Final Call to Purposeful Living

There's a version of reading a book like this where you finish it, feel genuinely moved and clear and motivated, and then slowly watch that clarity fade over the following weeks as the ordinary demands of life crowd back in. That version is extremely common. It's the insight-motivation-inconsistency-frustration cycle that the introduction described, and it's the cycle this entire book was designed to break.

The breaking happens not in the reading but in the doing. Specifically, in what you do today. Not tomorrow when you've had time to think about it. Not next Monday when the week starts fresh. Today, in the actual life you're living right now, with the actual resistance and complexity and imperfect conditions that are always present.

The leap into purposeful living isn't dramatic. It doesn't require a grand declaration or a complete overhaul of your daily structure. It requires one small, specific, values-connected action taken today with the internal chaos still present. One honest conversation you've been avoiding. One piece of work you've been delaying because the conditions haven't felt right. One moment of genuine presence with someone who matters to you, phone put away, attention fully there. One instance of feeling the anxiety and doing the thing anyway.

That one action is not small. It's the proof. The direct, lived, bodily proof that you don't have to wait for your internal world to cooperate before you can express what you value. Each piece of that proof compounds. Each time you act from your values in the presence of discomfort, you're building evidence that you're capable of it. And that evidence, accumulated over weeks and months, changes your relationship to difficulty at a level that no amount of understanding can reach on its own.

The clarity you want is available. The control you want, not control over your emotions, but control over your response to them, is available. The consistency you've been chasing, the kind that doesn't collapse when life gets hard, is available. Not as a permanent state you achieve and maintain effortlessly, but as a practiced capacity you return to, again and again, with increasing speed and decreasing drama each time.

The person you're capable of being isn't a future version of yourself waiting to emerge once you've solved all the internal problems. That person is already here. They're the one who noticed the thought without being controlled by it. The one who stayed with the difficult feeling instead of running. The one who chose the honest response when the defensive one was easier. You've already been that person in moments throughout this work. The task now is simply to make those moments more frequent, more deliberate, and more connected to the life you're actually trying to build.

Lasting resilience isn't built in the good weeks. It's built in the weeks where everything is hard and you show up anyway. Not because you feel like it. Because you've decided that what you value matters more than what you feel in any given moment. That decision, made repeatedly and specifically, in the ordinary moments of a real life, is what a profoundly fulfilling existence is actually made of.

Your Step-by-Step Action Plan for Life

Everything in this book, every concept, every practice, every case study and neuroscience explanation, was building toward something you can actually use in the moment. Not in theory. In the grocery store, the difficult meeting, the 2am spiral, the Tuesday afternoon when nothing feels meaningful and the old patterns are pulling hard. Here it is, as clearly and specifically as it can be stated.

Four steps. In sequence. Every time.

Step one: Observe the thought. When a difficult thought arrives, before you do anything else, pause and name it as a thought. Not "I'm going to fail at this" but "I'm having the thought that I'm going to fail at this." This takes three seconds. It creates the gap between you and the thought that everything else depends on. You're not arguing with the thought. You're not trying to replace it with a positive one. You're simply stepping back far enough to see it as a mental event rather than a fact. That step back is the beginning of everything. Practice it until it becomes your first response to any difficult thought, not your last resort.

Step two: Allow the feeling. Once you've observed the thought, turn toward whatever feeling is present in your body. Don't fight it. Don't flee it. Don't immediately reach for a technique to bring it down. Locate it physically. Describe its qualities in your head. Tight or loose, hot or cold, sharp or dull. Watch it the way you'd watch weather from inside a house. You're not the storm. You're the one observing it. The feeling is allowed to be there. It doesn't need to disappear before you can move. In fact, allowing it fully, without resistance, is often what allows it to move through faster than fighting it would. This step is the experiential expansion work made practical in a single moment. Feel it. Hold it. Don't run.

Step three: Check your compass. With the thought observed and the feeling allowed, ask one question. What do I value here? Not what do I want to feel. Not what would make the anxiety stop. What do I value in this specific situation? The honest communication. The quality of the work. The presence I want to offer. The commitment I made. Whatever it is, name it. This step is brief and it's everything. It redirects your attention from your internal weather to your direction. It transformations the question from "how am I feeling?" to "who am I being?" And that transformation is what makes the next step possible.

Step four: Take the action. Do the thing your values point toward. Not after the feeling clears. Not when you feel ready. Now, with the thought still present and the feeling still there. The smallest possible concrete step in the direction your values indicate. One sentence of the difficult email. The first thirty seconds of the hard conversation. The first line of the work you've been avoiding. You're not waiting for alignment before you act. You're creating alignment through the act. The action doesn't need to be perfect. It needs to be real. It needs to happen today, in the actual conditions you're in, not in the ideal conditions you're waiting for.

Those four steps are the entire model made portable. Observe the thought. Allow the feeling. Check your compass. Take the action. You can do this in thirty seconds. You can do it in the middle of a meeting, a conflict, a moment of self-doubt, a wave of anxiety before something that matters. You can do it when the internal chaos is loud and the old patterns are pulling hard. It doesn't require perfect conditions. It doesn't require you to be in a calm, centered state first. It requires only the decision to use it.

Print those four steps. Put them on your desk, your bathroom mirror, your phone case. Not as decoration. As a functional reference for the moments when you need them most, which are always the moments when they're hardest to remember.

The four steps work because they address the complete sequence of what happens when you're pulled toward reactive functioning. The thought arrives and threatens to fuse with your sense of reality. Step one defuses it. The feeling arrives and threatens to overwhelm your capacity to choose. Step two expands your tolerance for it. The urgency of the moment threatens to crowd out your sense of direction. Step three restores it. And the gap between knowing and doing threatens to keep you in place. Step four closes it.

Every time you complete this sequence, you're practicing transcendent functioning. Not as an abstract ideal. As a specific, embodied, real-time skill. And every repetition strengthens the neural pathways that make it more accessible the next time. Your brain is literally being reorganized around this sequence with each use. The practice is changing you at a level that goes deeper than conscious understanding.

One final thing, and it's the most important thing in this entire conclusion. You always have the power to choose your response. Not the power to choose which thoughts arise. Not the power to choose which feelings show up. Not the power to control what other people do or what circumstances present themselves. But the power to choose your response to all of it. That power is not conditional on your emotional state. It's not dependent on having slept well or feeling motivated or being in the right headspace. It's available in every moment, including this one, including the hardest ones, including the ones where it feels most completely unavailable. That power is what this book has been about.

Not giving it to you, because it was always yours. Helping you see it clearly, build it deliberately, and use it consistently in the only place it's ever available: the present moment of your actual life.The four steps are your permanent reference. The values are your compass. The practices are your foundation. And the choice, made again and again in the ordinary moments of a real and imperfect life, is yours.

Glossary

Authentic Fulfillment: A state of deep satisfaction and well-being arising from living in alignment with one's core values and purpose.

Cognitive Flexibility: The mental ability to switch between thinking about two different concepts, or to think about multiple concepts simultaneously.

Emotional Resilience: The capacity to recover quickly from difficulties; toughness.

Integration: The process of incorporating various aspects of the self, including thoughts, emotions, experiences, and beliefs, into a cohesive whole.

Mindful Awareness: A state of active, open attention on the present, without judgment.

Psychological Flexibility: The ability to contact the present moment fully and, based on what the situation affords, persist with or change behavior in the service of chosen values.

Purpose: An emergent quality that arises from conscious alignment with deeply held values, guiding actions and providing meaning.

Self-Compassion: The quality of being concerned about one's own suffering and being moved to try to relieve it.

Transcendent Functioning: A dynamic process of cultivating presence and purpose, integrating the self, and fostering psychological flexibility to achieve authentic fulfillment and resilience.

Values: Core principles that guide one's actions and give life meaning.

References

Abramowitz, J. S. (2006). The psychological treatment of obsessive–compulsive disorder. *Canadian Journal of Psychiatry, 51*(7), 407–416.

Barlow, D. H. (2002). *Anxiety and its disorders: The nature and treatment of anxiety and panic* (2nd ed.). Guilford Press.

Baumeister, R. F., Vohs, K. D., & Tice, D. M. (2007). The strength model of self-control. *Current Directions in Psychological Science, 16*(6), 351–355.

Beck, A. T. (1976). *Cognitive therapy and the emotional disorders*. International Universities Press.

Breines, J. G., & Chen, S. (2012). Self-compassion increases self-improvement motivation. *Personality and Social Psychology Bulletin, 38*(9), 1133–1143.

Brewer, J. A., Worhunsky, P. D., Gray, J. R., Tang, Y. Y., Weber, J., & Kober, H. (2011). Meditation experience is associated with differences in default mode network activity and connectivity. *Proceedings of the National Academy of Sciences, 108*(50), 20254–20259.

Brickman, P., & Campbell, D. T. (1971). Hedonic relativism and planning the good society. In M. H. Appley (Ed.), *Adaptation-level theory: A symposium* (pp. 287–302). Academic Press.

Chawla, N., & Ostafin, B. (2007). Experiential avoidance as a functional dimensional approach to psychopathology: An empirical review. *Journal of Clinical Psychology, 63*(9), 871–890.

Clear, J. (2018). *Atomic habits: An easy & proven way to build good habits & break bad ones*. Avery.

Csikszentmihalyi, M. (2009). *Flow: The psychology of optimal experience*. Harper Perennial Modern Classics.

Davidson, R. J., & McEwen, B. S. (2012). Social influences on neuroplasticity: Stress and interventions to promote well-being. *Nature Neuroscience, 15*(5), 689–695.

Diener, E., Lucas, R. E., & Scollon, C. N. (2006). Beyond the hedonic treadmill: Revising the adaptation theory of well-being. *American Psychologist, 61*(4), 305–314.

Doidge, N. (2007). *The brain that changes itself:*

Stories of personal triumph from the frontiers of brain science. Viking.

Doran, G. T. (1981). There's a S.M.A.R.T. way to write management's goals and objectives. *Management Review, 70*(11), 35–36.

Dugas, M. J., & Robichaud, M. (2007). *Cognitive-behavioral treatment for generalized anxiety disorder: From science to practice*. Routledge.

Flavell, J. H. (1979). Metacognition and cognitive monitoring: A new area of cognitive–developmental inquiry. *American Psychologist, 34*(10), 906–911.

Frankl, V. E. (2006). *Man's search for meaning*. Beacon Press. *(Original work published 1946)*

Gross, J. J. (1998). The emerging field of emotion regulation: An integrative review. *Review of General Psychology, 2*(3), 271–299.

Gross, J. J. (2015). Emotion regulation: Current status and future prospects. *Psychological Inquiry, 26*(1), 1–26.

Hayes, S. C., Luoma, J. B., Bond, F. W., Masuda,

A., & Lillis, J. (2006). Acceptance and commitment therapy: Model, processes and outcomes. *Behaviour Research and Therapy, 44*(1), 1–25.

Hayes, S. C., Wilson, K. G., Gifford, E. V., Follette, V. M., & Strosahl, K. (1996). Experimental avoidance and behavioral disorders: A functional dimensional approach to diagnosis and treatment. *Journal of Consulting and Clinical Psychology, 64*(6), 1152–1168.

Hölzel, B. K., Carmody, J., Vangel, M., Congleton, C., Yerramsetti, S. M., Gard, T., & Lazar, S. W. (2011). Mindfulness practice leads to increases in regional brain gray matter density. *Psychiatry Research: Neuroimaging, 191*(1), 36–43.

Kabat-Zinn, J. (2003). Mindfulness-based interventions in context: Past, present, and future. *Clinical Psychology: Science and Practice, 10*(2), 144–156.

Kashdan, T. B., Barrios, V., Forsyth, J. P., & Steger, M. F. (2006). Experiential avoidance as a generalized psychological vulnerability: Comparisons with coping and emotion regulation strategies. *Behaviour Research and Therapy, 44*(9), 1301–1320.

Lazar, S. W., Kerr, C. E., Wasserman, R. H., Gray, J. R., Greve, D. N., Treadway, M. T., McGarvey, M., Quinn, B. T., Dusek, J. A., Benson, H., Rauch, S. L., Moore, C. I., & Fischl, B. (2005). Meditation experience is associated with increased cortical thickness. *NeuroReport, 16*(17), 1893–1897.

LeDoux, J. E. (1996). *The emotional brain: The mysterious underpinnings of emotional life.* Simon & Schuster.

Lieberman, M. D., Eisenberger, N. I., Crockett, M. J., Tom, S. M., Pfeifer, J. H., & Way, B. M. (2007). Putting feelings into words: Affect labeling disrupts amygdala activity in response to affective stimuli. *Psychological Science, 18*(5), 421–428.

Marlatt, G. A., & Gordon, J. R. (1985). *Relapse prevention: Maintenance strategies in the treatment of addictive behaviors.* Guilford Press.

Neff, K. D. (2003). Self-compassion: An alternative conceptualization of a healthy attitude toward oneself. *Self and Identity, 2*(2), 85–101.

Raichle, M. E., MacLeod, A. M., Snyder, A. Z., Powers, W. J., Gusnard, D. A., & Shulman, G. L. (2001). A default mode of brain function.

Proceedings of the National Academy of Sciences, 98(2), 676–682.

Wegner, D. M. (1994). Ironic processes of mental control. *Psychological Review, 101*(1), 34–52.

Wenzlaff, R. M., & Wegner, D. M. (2000). Thought suppression. *Annual Review of Psychology, 51*, 59–91.

www.ingramcontent.com/pod-product-compliance
Lightning Source LLC
LaVergne TN
LVHW040514210926
848480LV00005BA/1453